SCHUBERT, THE MAN

42405

OSCAR BIE

SCHUBERT
THE MAN

GP

GREENWOOD PRESS, PUBLISHERS
WESTPORT, CONNECTICUT

Originally published in 1928
by Dodd, Mead & Company, New York

First Greenwood Reprinting 1971

Library of Congress Catalogue Card Number 76-109710

SBN 8371-4201-6

Printed in the United States of America

ACKNOWLEDGMENT

The publishers are indebted to the *Musical Courier* for its courtesy in granting permission to use the illustrations which appear in this volume.

TRANSLATOR'S NOTE

For invaluable aid in completing the latter half of this book, the translator is indebted to Judith Heller-Bernays of Vienna.

J. S. U.

FOREWORD

The international character of the Schubert Centenary makes it opportune to present this biographical work by Oscar Bie, translated into English. Intrinsically the book is an admirable study of Schubert the man, combining sympathy with scholarship. It possesses additional weight as the Centennial biography, since it fills the long-felt want for a non-technical study, competent on the musical side and in scope wide enough to merit the interest and appreciation of the layman.

Mr. Bie's literary distinction and musical knowledge have been amply demonstrated in his books on the opera, the dance, and the history of music —the majority of which have been translated into English.

I believe this book will have lasting value, yet I would not underestimate its immediate and far-reaching application as the Centennial biography, approved by the International Advisory Body. The Schubert Centenary is a tribute not limited to any class or group. Especially in America has the commemoration taken a civic and educational scope, in which musical and art societies are supplemented by community forces comprising the schools, the churches, and Industry.

FOREWORD

The Centennial biography will, no doubt, advance a just appraisal of Schubert the man and his works. To commend it to English-speaking readers is, I believe, to render a service.

LOUIS STERLING
Chairman, Committee on
International Relations
Schubert Centenary

INTRODUCTION

The celebration of the Schubert Centennial in America is being carried out with broad thoroughness and purposeful vision. One of its fruits is this biography, which aims at being both a characteristic study of the man and a treatise on the music of one of the greatest, most appealing, and most beloved of composers.

On behalf of the Schubert Centennial Committee, I take pleasure in commending this book to American readers.

OTTO H. KAHN
Chairman, Advisory Body
Schubert Centennial

CONTENTS

ILLUSTRATIONS

ILLUSTRATIONS

[xvi]

ILLUSTRATIONS

SCHUBERT, THE MAN

HIS LIFE

THAT face! At first it has the look of a school-master, glancing through his spectacles with friendly eyes. But it is clear that this is the face of one who has mastered his craft. He died so young—at thirty-one, when many are just beginning—and so few of his compositions appeared during his life that the printing of his collected works covered a period longer than his whole earthly existence. Whom the gods love, die young. But why should I quote that? If he had lived, he would have projected the distinction of his youth into a still riper manhood—into an indescribably fruitful future—and would have become the first and foremost of all.

It is the face of a teacher, but not of a strict one. The hair curls about the brow. No, this is no pedagogue; this is an artist, a true musician, certainly, if not a virtuoso. The gaze is modest; it betokens a man of the people, one who can work and play man to man, one who can casually create beautiful things. The mouth is slightly sensual, with a look of friendly expectancy, a hint of gaiety. The lips smile; they seem ready to tell stories, new and endless stories or the old stories with new varia-

tions, never tiring in their Viennese *Gemütlichkeit.*[1] There is nothing commanding, scheming,
nothing pressing, nothing problematical. All flows
naturally from heart to heart, the sense of it
scarcely touching the encompassing world. Love
encircles you, and will bring mankind to you for a
thousand years, over a space so great that your
dreams could never have imagined it. From the
thin and meagre soil of an uneventful life there
blossoms a strength that will endure.

Dance and song are the sources of your power:
the lightly swinging melody, the gentle harmony,
the cradling rhythm. There are no convulsions, no
sudden descent or soaring between dramatic contrasts. The listener to your music moves in a landscape full of sun and fragrance, a landscape of
spring, on a day when music is first being created,
when man is still at one with himself, grateful for
his surroundings, without mutiny or passion. The
powers themselves have not been differentiated. It
is a world of youth and faith, but also a world of
age and escape; for it is the privilege of age that it
can regain an almost untroubled country.

The delicate sensuousness, the lyric playfulness
(that only in the later works bears certain witness

[1] Literally translated this word means: "easy sociability." But all suggestion of charm is lost by this exactitude. *Gemütlichkeit* is such an
integrated part of the language that it loses, if not its life, at least its
character by translation.

[2]

of the Dæmonic) flow easily and quietly. He plays, composes, improvises indefatigably. He's at his manuscripts night and day. He stretches the same themes wider and wider. There is no end to the continuity and broadening.

And yet the length is never clumsy or unnatural, for it is the very breath of a musical spirit that is born for the varied and voluble expression of ideas. This spirit, never suffering confusion, opens the sluices of its stone-stream, looses the flood, swinging, plashing, overleaping itself. It is as though the heart were happily opened and the blood poured itself out unrestrained, unhindered by scholarship or rules.

And how amazing! This creator, who did not need to restrain himself from the flood of his thoughts, his fancies, his forms; who dared to allow himself playfulness for its own sake; he, as if from a very superfluity of the long line, was the first to understand how to set the short phrases. He was the discoverer in music of the short lyric, which, in a few lines and turns of a phrase, catches and contains a mood. Are these impromptus his essence? Are they the source of his creativeness? Are the longer pieces only the joining together of such short and unconnected thoughts? It may be. In this way we come nearer him. Tradition and scholarship lay in his pen; structure and variation

[3]

belonged to the style of his time; but the quiet limpid character of a locked mood, the pastoral in music, that was his genius, his discovery, his fruitfulness, and his gratitude to nature. From this standpoint all is clear; speculations draw towards this central point, and all conclusions proceed from this discovery.

Let us examine his different genres. There is none that is foreign to him, but there are certain ones that are native. Piano-music, song, and the small orchestra are his province. A little symphonic music might be added, and a fragment of opera. But the last is not his particular characteristic. His art is intimate. Where Beethoven, at the same period, projected works in large dimensions away from their center, Schubert condensed everything, from a smaller circle, and drew it into himself. Bach, also, in his own way, was intimate, but one might say that Bach's intimacy was in the nature of metaphysical service; Schubert's was a private thing, responsible only to himself.

There is little to tell of his life, which is thin in incident compared with his rich and exuberant talents. Everything went inward. The biographer must devote himself quietly to Schubert's art, which surpasses any drama of his life, and finds completion in its own contemplation. If it was not recognized sufficiently then, it is recognized to the full now, since it has become a part of ourselves.

All romantic streams of music flow from this source. The best German essentials lie rooted in this landscape. Noise is silenced, struggle is stilled, problems sleep; here blooms a new, unsuspected, and unmeasured tenderness, the gentle love of music.

He was a teacher's son and a teacher. He was born on January 31, 1797, in Lichtenthal near Vienna, where his father taught. His father and his brothers were musical, and he grew up in a propitious atmosphere. From his father he learned to play the violin, from his brother the piano; and then he was given over to Herr Holzer, the choral director of the Lichtenthal district church, with whom he learned theory and organ-playing and cultivated a good soprano voice. At that time a general musical training was as usual as it is now unusual. He learned quickly and easily and soon outstripped his teachers. Then the great event occurred. He was admitted into the Guild of the Court Singers, which necessitated visits to the Convent and Gymnasium and gave him the opportunity to take part in a small orchestra formed by the pupils. When he was about thirteen years old the impulse to compose awoke powerfully. His father at first opposed it, as has been the case with

[5]

most fathers of geniuses. But young Franz let nothing disturb him, procured music-paper wherever
possible, and when he had none ruled himself some
on any white sheet, and wrote and wrote and
wrote. This made his father angry. Then Franz
studied with Salieri, after the musical director of
the convent had become devilishly watchful of
him. What could the good Salieri teach him? He
was a courtier, musically very modest, not even
ripe for Mozart and Beethoven, an intrigant, often
against his own pupils.

At this time, in November 1812, Franz wrote
to his brother Ferdinand: "Out at once with what
lies on my heart. And so I'll come sooner to my
goal and you'll not be detained by nice digressions.
For a long time I've considered my condition, and,
taken all in all, found it good; but here and there
it could be bettered. You know from experience
that a man would often like to eat a roll and a
couple of apples, especially when, after a poor din-
ner, he can look forward to eight and a half empty
hours, followed by a poor supper. This often very
pressing wish recurs increasingly and, *nolens vo-
lens*, I must at last make a change. The few pennies
that I get from Father go to the devil in the first
few days. What shall I do the rest of the time?
Frankly, I'm not ashamed to call on you. (Matthew
Chap. 11–4.) So I thought: How would it be if you

would send me a couple of Kreutzer every month?
You'd hardly notice it, while I would feel happy
in my cell and would be contented. As I said, I
supported myself with the words of the Apostle
Matthew who said: 'He who has two coats, let him
give one to the poor.' With which I hope you will
agree and respond to your loving, poverty-stricken,
hopeful, and once more indigent brother—Franz."

His father considered it all and became amiable
again. People assured him that Franz was something out of the ordinary. Family quartettes were
played at home, which helped the boy greatly. His
friend Spaun took him to the opera. He saw there
for the first time the singer Michael Vogl, who was
to become his good fortune. Gluck's *Iphigenia in
Tauris* delighted him the most. Anna Milder sang
it. He sat with Spaun and Theodor Körner in the
restaurant "Blumenstöckl" (The Flower Pot)—
and the three celebrated their enthusiasm for
Gluck in such a way that they were almost drawn
into a quarrel with a University professor whose
intelligence was not satisfied by Gluck.

What next? The fourteen-year-old military
service threatened. One is free from this service
only if one is a teacher. His father said—"How
would it be, Franz, if you became a teacher, like
myself?" Franz considered: "Then I'd be free of
the convent—this prison—and could surely fol-

low my leaning." Therefore he studied pedagogy and at seventeen passed his examinations as coming assistant. He received his diploma. In most subjects he was good; average in the chief studies, the elements of pedagogy and Latin writing, less good in theoretical theology and in mathematics, and quite poor in practical religion. At that time a distinction was made between theoretical and practical knowledge, but not between officials and men. One who had a real understanding of men was the poet Johann Mayrhofer, ten years older than Schubert, a book-censor who had been given the office against his wish. "My friendship with Schubert," he relates, "was begun by a friend of my youth, who gave Schubert a poem of mine, 'Am See,' to set to music. In company with this friend, Schubert entered the room which five years later we were to share together. It was in a gloomy street. The building, inside and out, had felt the weight of time; the roof was sunken, the light cut off by a large building opposite. A played-out piano, a small bookshelf—such was the room in which hours were passed that will never leave my memory." He lived in Schubert's songs and carried them as possessions during all his days. A friendly circle was created.

Schubert's life has been written in many books —most extensively in the biography of Walter

Franz Schubert's father.
From an unsigned painting in the Schubert Museum

Front view and courtyard of Schubert's birthplace

Dahms, which appeared in 1912 and surpassed all earlier works, since it was based on the mass of authentic material collected in Vienna with such industry by Alois Fellner. I can not invent new facts and thanks for the old ones must be given to Dahms' book. Nor can the arrangement be much altered. Everything is as clear as it is beautiful. It is enough for me to share in a loving service to this good being.

In 1814, Franz became a primary teacher. It is easy to imagine how that suited him! Still, instead of being obliged to don the colored coat of the militia he could often quaff a convivial glass with his friends and write all the music that occurred to him. He received a state pension of forty gulden a year; nevertheless he wrote the "Erlkönig."

Spaun tells of this in his *Memoirs:* "One afternoon I went with Mayrhofer to visit Schubert, who lived at that time with his father at Himmelpfortgrunde.[1] We found Schubert glowing, reading the 'Erlkönig' aloud from a book. He kept walking to and fro, the book in his hand. Suddenly he sat down, and in an incredibly short time the noble ballad was on paper. As Schubert had no piano we ran with it to the Convent, and there, on the same evening, the 'Erlkönig' was sung and hailed with

---

[1] The district, picturesquely called "The Gate of Heaven," which no longer exists under this name.

enthusiasm. The old court organist, Ruzicka, then played it over without the voice, sympathetically and attentively, and was deeply moved by the composition. When one or two wanted to strike out the often-recurring dissonances, Ruzicka, sounding them on the piano, showed how they corresponded with the text, how much more beautiful they were, and how happily they resolved."

In the matter of memoirs, one can never be certain that everything tallies. Still, even though the "Erlkönig" may have been completed earlier than this account shows, it marks Schubert's first great step towards the heights of art. It signifies his entry into a larger world, and is a proof of creative power rather than a proof of erudition.

This brings us to the end of the year 1815. At this time Anselm Hüttenbrenner joined the friendly circle which met at Salieri's. At first, Franz distrusted him and thought he would be only a superficial acquaintance. Then to his surprise he found that Hüttenbrenner preferred the same places in his work that he himself thought best. This understanding brought them closer together. At Mozatti's they sang with their host and Aszmayer every Thursday, self-harmonized Quartettes which Schubert wrote extemporaneously, the casual flowering of old, intimate music!

On the feminine side he was less successful. Her

name was Therese Grob; she had sung the soprano
solo in his first Mass; pockmarks were her jewels
but she loved his music beyond everything. He
approached her parents. He wrote several pieces
for her and her brother. Schubert remarked to
Hüttenbrenner on a walk, "She isn't pretty, but
she is good—truly good." She would have ac-
cepted him if he had had any situation. But he
found none. He tried several things, but they came
to nothing, and, since the good Therese did not
wish to wait any longer, she married a baker. Schubert wrote in his diary: "Marriage in this time is a
dreadful thought for a single man. He wavers between melancholy or the coarsest sensuality." And
from then on he ceased to concern himself seri-
ously with women.

Things were going badly. An amateur orchestra
gave him some comfort, and a couple of music-
lessons eked out his existence, but without his
friends he would have gone under. First his
friends tried an appeal to Goethe. As he himself
was far too modest to turn to the god at Weimar,
his friends had him neatly copy out his finest
Goethe songs. Spaun packed them up and composed the following script to go with them: "The
poems gathered together in the present notebook
were set to music by a nineteen-year-old composer
named Franz Schubert, to whom nature has given

a decided ability for composition since his tenderest childhood. Salieri, the Nestor of musicians, with an unselfish love for art, has brought this talent to fruition. The general approval which these songs, as well as other finished works, have won for the young artist from the severest judges in the art,·as well as from those not connoisseurs, from men as well as from women, together with the general wish of his friends, at last moves the modest youth to open his musical career by publishing a part of his compositions. In humility, the young artist hopes he may dare dedicate this collection to your Excellency, to whose noble poesy he not only assigns the existence of a great part of them, but also thanks his development as a German singer. Being too modest to deem his work worthy to bear the great honor of the vast riches of the German tongue, or to carry your highly celebrated name on his brow, he has not the courage to ask your Excellency for this great privilege; and I—one of his friends—have urged—" But I can go no further with this dripping flattery that was well-meant but missed its mark. His Excellency answered not a word. In 1822, Max Löwenthal visited Goethe and talked to him about Schubert. Goethe knew nothing of him. At a much later date, Schröder-Devrient sang the "Erlkönig" for Goethe. He believed he had heard the song before when it expressed nothing to him. "So rendered (he admitted) the whole now formed a clear picture."

The second attempt was with the publishers. Spaun wrote to Breitkopf and Härtel and sent the "Erlkönig"—as a trial. The publisher suspected a hoax through the misuse of the name of a Dresden composer, another Franz Schubert. He sent the "Erlkönig" to the latter and asked for an explanation. The other Schubert answered: "I never composed the Erlkönig cantata, but I'll seek to find out who has perpetrated this clumsy fraud, and to discover the culprit who has so misused my name." The real composer, however, received no answer.

Help finally came from a singer. This must be emphasized—not from a great poet, not from a great publisher, but really, for once, from a great singer. Vogl was uncommonly famous and was known to be difficult of approach. This time, Friend Schober pulled the trick. He had himself introduced to Vogl and went into ecstasies over Schubert. Vogl shook his head. He had enough of this eternal music; young people were always being recommended, but nothing ever came of it. When this was reported to Schubert he said: "I did not expect anything else." But his friend would not give up, and at last Vogl visited Schubert one evening to see, as he said, what there was to it. Spaun tells it all: "Vogl, very pompous; Schubert, small and unimposing. He made an awkward curtsy and stammered something about the honor of the acquaintance. Vogl wrinkled his nose and finally said, 'Well, let's see what you've got. Accompany me.' It was Mayrhofer's 'Augenlied.' Vogl hummed it over and said, somewhat coldly, 'not bad.' He tried out a few more songs and said to Schubert, at his departure, 'There is something in you, but you are too little the comedian, too little the charlatan. You waste your beautiful ideas without making a proper show of them.' However, he could not dismiss the pieces from his mind, but grew continually fonder of the songs. Unsought, he returned to Schubert, invited Schubert to his house and studied with him. Finally, in an intoxication of enthusiasm, it struck him that he would become Schubert's prophet. A quiet creation came to the light of day. Schubert wrote in a letter: 'The manner in which Vogl sings and I accompany, the way we in this moment seem to be one, is something new and unheard of to these people.' "

At the end of 1817, Schubert took a vacation from his post as teacher. The danger of military service being over, he wanted to see how far music alone could take him. In the next year one of his compositions was publicly performed for the first time. The violinist Jaell arranged a concert in "The Roman Emperor," in which one of Schubert's

overtures was played. We read with satisfaction a
contemporary criticism in one of the Vienna
theatre papers which reports that Schubert moved
and dazed all hearts with happy surprise. With further satisfaction, we read from his biography that
Dr. Sartori, Mayrhofer's senior, for the first time
printed a song of Schubert's as a supplement to the
*Picturesque Pocket Edition for Friends of the More
Interesting Surroundings and Natural Artistic
Wonders of the Austrian Monarchy.* The title of
the song was "Erlafsee," and the poem was Mayrhofer's. Still a third star showed itself. Schubert
was recommended as piano teacher for both daughters of Count Esterhazy. In winter they lived in
Vienna, in summer on their Hungarian estate,
Zelesz. He received two guldens per hour; he went
with them in summer and listened to the melodies
of the Gypsies; but he wrote to his brother Ferdinand: "Things aren't going well with you—I
wish I could change places with you, so that you
could once be happy . . . as well as things are
with me, healthy though I am, in spite of the good
people that are here, still I shall be endlessly glad
for that instant which means—back to Vienna!
Yes, beloved Vienna, you shut the dearest and best
in your narrow space, and only seeing you again
can still this longing."

Gradually shadows lowered; he was treated as a

hireling and placed outside the company. Perhaps the Countess was the only one who had an interest for the reality of art. He lived at the lodge. Near by, forty geese gabbled so that one could not hear one's own words; besides which the keeper was "highly musical" and played two dances on the lute. Schubert would like to be friendly with his son. He prefers the surgeon, a jolly greybeard, seventy-five years old. But he announces in his letters that the cook, the ladies' maid, the chambermaid, the nurse, the doorman and two stable masters are his daily associates. How he suffered under this bigotry! He said "bigoted as an old harlot, dumb as a brass donkey, obstinate as a buffalo. It is a pleasure to hear the priest shout from the pulpit, 'hussies,' 'dogs,' etc. He places a skull on the pulpit and says: 'Here stands your pockmarked mug. This is the way you will look one of these days.' "

He came back to Vienna and gave instruction at the Esterhazys', for the time being, only in winter. School? No, that did not exist any longer. Never again would it exist for him. His father was very angry. Bohemianism bloomed. Now he roomed with Schober, now with Mayrhofer. Moritz von Schwind, gay, friendly, talkative, romantic as Schubert himself, entered the friendly circle. If any one came to him during the day, he relates, Schubert only said: "God greet you. How are you?" and kept writing; whereupon the visitor disappeared. Evenings they foregathered at the "Hungarian Crown," and relished the labors of the day. The manuscripts lay everywhere, and no one troubled about them. Schubert sang them to his friends; they took the notebooks along with them and did not return them. Joseph Hüttenbrenner, Anselm's brother, obliging servitor to Schubert's genius, gathered them together and arranged them carefully in a drawer; but then the place got into an untidy state again, and Schubert affirmed it was not such a bad state, as there were only a few songs that really pleased him.

Seldom did diversion beckon him away from Vienna. This summer he took his first journey with Vogl, who asked him to go along. They paddled about in Upper Austria. The "Forellen" (Trout) Quintette was written. Good modest Schubert! When anyone wrote to ask him for a composition, he answered: "Since I do not possess anything for full orchestra that I could send into the world with an easy conscience, and since there exist so many pieces by great masters (for instance Beethoven's Overtures to Prometheus, Coriolanus, Egmont, and so forth), I must cordially beg your forgiveness that I am not able to serve you at this moment, as it would be a detriment for me to appear with something mediocre."

Nevertheless he experimented with music for a farce. Vogl recommended his "Zwillingsbrüder" (Twin Brothers) to the theatre next to the Kärntnerthor, and himself sang the chief part. Anselm Hüttenbrenner relates that it was a great success. Schubert was stormily called for, but did not appear because his coat was in too bad a condition. Anselm took off his own swallow-tails and pressed Schubert to put it on. But it was useless. The manager came forward and announced that Schubert was not present, and Schubert, hearing this, smiled. In the same year he appeared at the Theater-ander-Wien with his second work, "Die Zauberharfe" (The Magic Harp). He should have received a recompense of five-hundred gulden, but the manager went bankrupt.

Leopold Sonnleithner then became his "angel," and brought him to Fröhlichs. Four daughters, Katharina, Anna, Barbara, and Josepha, comprised the household. Sonnleithner, a cousin of Grillparzer, brought them songs from a young man, reported to be very good. Kathi sat down and tried them. An official, whose avocation was singing, shouted: "That is something quite extraordinary. Let's have a look." He sang the songs, and Schu-

[18]

Room in which the composer probably was born

Room in the Schubert Museum with the composer's piano

Schubert at the age of sixteen

bert himself followed close after. That was a musical house. Kathi was the beloved of Grillparzer,
who said of her "she gets drunk on music." How
charming it must have been there. We still have
pictures of the sisters. They do all honor to their
name. Kathi said of Schubert, "He was a noble soul,
never envious or jealous; and whenever he heard
anything beautiful in music he laid his hands together over his mouth and sat there quite ecstatic."
When he had composed something new, he came
to the girls, seated himself on the sofa and said
happily: "Today I have made something that I
really believe has succeeded."

To understand Schubert fully, a person must feel
about him this Viennese air, this friendliness and
gaiety that bloomed luxuriously from the soil of an
intricately interwoven officialdom. Inspiration does
not proceed from the great world into the narrow
city. It steps softly from the quiet heart, from the
repressed emotion, to accustom the world to itself,
to charm it, and to give itself to the world—to alter
its very spirit.

In 1821, the friendly circle loosened. Schubert
separated himself from Mayrhofer. They must
have quarrelled fearfully. Mayrhofer was often
irascible and finally unbearable. He went rapidly
downhill. He is said to have sought death unsuccessfully in the Danube. Then, in 1836, he threw

himself from his office window and was killed. Bauernfeld, when he heard of it, remarked—"A sacrifice to the Austrian temperament." Hüttenbrenner and Spaun moved away, and that meant more to Schubert than it seems when it is related today. He lived only in this friendly exchange. In their stead, Kupelwieser and Schwind, poor painters, came close to him. There were several public performances of his works. The "Erlkönig" was sung, in an opera house concert, with telling effect, by Vogl. "Das Dörfchen" (The Village) and "Der Gesang der Geister über dem Wasser" (The Song of the Spirits over the Water) were also given. The "Erlkönig" had to be repeated. Hüttenbrenner accompanied Vogl, and Schubert, who was just as well able to play the accompaniment, turned the pages. But there were not many such concerts and soon they ceased altogether. Leopold Sonnleithner had provided the one in the opera for him. Sonnleithner's uncle Joseph had helped found the Society of Noble Ladies for the Promotion of the Good and Useful, and this Society arranged the concert. Joseph's brother, Ignaz, Court-Agent, Notary, Writer, Professor of the Laws of Exchange, and a splendid bass, occupied a wonderful apartment on the Bauernmarkt, where he could assemble a hundred and twenty people. There was always a concert on Friday evenings, and these

[20]

concerts became so crowded that finally entrance cards had to be given out. Leopold, the son of Ignaz, was the first real Schubert fanatic. He made a collection of copies of Schubert's songs. From 1819 on, Schubert frequented the Sonnleithner house and was always encouraged. Finally, Leopold had a brilliant idea. The publishers had always laid the Schubertian songs aside because the accompaniment was so difficult, and the composer too little known. Now matters should be changed. Father Ignaz, with a small syndicate, should advance the printing expenses of the first collection; a publisher should take over the labor; the second collection should be brought out from the proceeds of the first, and so on, *ad lib.* It succeeded. The first books were dedicated to persons of high standing, and they responded with an honorarium. With every edition, appeared new advertising, which stimulated the sales. "Because of constant demand, the publishers are compelled to bring out these two volumes and present them to the friends of German Song. The choice of poems already denotes the ingenious temper of the composer, but the way he grasps the poetic masterpieces and expresses them musically uncovers the extraordinary genius of the young artist." One copy was dedicated to the poet Ladislaus Pryker, the Patriarch of Venice. He replied: "Highly-honoured Sir—Your kind announcement that you have dedicated the fourth volume of your incomparable songs to me gives me the greater pleasure since it will remind me the more often of that evening when I was so gripped by the deep expressions of your spirit—particularly by the tones of your 'Wanderer.' I am proud to belong with you to one and the same fatherland, and sign myself, with the greatest respect, Yours sincerely, L. Pryker-Patriarch." And, at this, his father ceased to be angry.

He tried everything. He worked with Schober on an opera, "Alfonso and Estrella." He was given hope that it might be performed in Vienna. Also Dresden was suggested, where Weber might interest himself. But, as usual, it came to nothing. This work was first performed by Liszt in Weimar in 1854. Today it's quite dead. Joseph Hüttenbrenner literally tore himself apart for Schubert in a business way, but all in vain. What more can be told of him at this time? He wrote the B Minor symphony, from which he heard just as little as from any other of his symphonies. And he wrote the "Wanderer-Phantasie" for the piano, which proved somewhat difficult to play, even for himself. He tried to approach Beethoven. He dedicated to *The Great Man,* as his "votary and admirer," the Eight Variations on a French Theme, for four hands, that were published as Opus 10. He took a copy in his hand and went to Beethoven. What a decision that must have been! But he had not announced himself; the Master was not there, and so he left the copy behind with a servant. It is certain that Beethoven found the Variations very good, and played them often with his nephew Karl. But the result was nil.

Joseph Hüttenbrenner had also turned to the Publisher, Peters. He wanted to see if there was not a more general interest in Schubert. Then the answer from Peters was received. In an evasive fashion he said he was so occupied with Spohr, Rombert and Hummel that he had little time left for young authors. Nevertheless, Schubert had a very decent income from his Viennese publishers. Altogether, up to this time, it was two thousand gulden, to which the "Erlkönig" had contributed the most. Sonnleithner's plan, that had been so cleverly thought out, ran along very successfully. But no one had reckoned with Schubert's own business ignorance. One day his publisher said to him: "Why do you want to keep on reckoning with an uncertain income? Sell me the plates and the rights for eight hundred Gulden and then you will know what you have." And Schubert agreed —thereby threatening his whole existence. How could any one help him? He had so many friends and consulted none of them. He could have lived comfortably; he could have demanded greater honorariums. Now that was a thing of the past.

Then he became ill and he lost his hair. Doctors may decide what was the cause of his illness and his early death. He had sometimes lived rather loosely. Who knows what may have resulted? The failure of the opera was real to him. Also the misfortune with his friends was real. Schober even became an actor. A great deal was torn asunder. Poor Schubert often had to scratch for himself something besides notes. He wrote poems, in the characteristic taste of the time. He wrote a sort of parable of his life "Mein Traum" (My Dream), baroque and pompous. He also wrote a Diary. In March 1824, we find this entry: "No one understands the pain of another, no one another's joy. Men hope to be brought together, close to each other, but they travel in parallels, away from each other. O misery for him who understands this! What I have produced in music exists because of my understanding and my pain. Those compositions which pain alone produced seem to please the world most." Shortly after he wrote, "O fantasy! highest treasure of mankind, you inexhaustible Source from which artists as well as sages drink, remain with us, even if recognized and honored by few, in order to save us from so-called enlightenment, that hateful skele-

[24]

ton without flesh and blood!" Gloomy is this March, 1824. He wrote to Kupelwieser in Rome: "At last I can again pour out my soul to someone. You are so good and trustworthy. You will surely excuse me for things others would take in bad part. In a word, I feel myself the unhappiest, most miserable being on the earth. Consider a person whose health will never be right, and who, from his desperation over this fact, makes it worse instead of better. Think of a man, I say, whose shining hopes have come to nothing; to whom the fortune of love and friendship offers nothing but pain; from whom the inspiration of the beautiful, at least creatively, threatens to disappear—and ask yourself if such a one is not a miserable, unhappy being? 'My peace is gone—my heart is heavy—I shall never find it again'—so I could say every day —since every night that I go to sleep I hope nevermore to awake; and each morning yesterday's sorrow greets me anew. So, joyless and friendless, I pass my days; and if Schwind did not visit me occasionally and bring me a beam from those sweet days that have passed . . ."

It is the epoch of the "Müller Lieder" (Miller's Songs). He dedicated them to the splendid tenor Karl von Schönstein, whom he had met at Esterhazy's, and who had become his new prophet, quicker and more sincere than Vogl. He went once again, with Schönstein, to pass the summer at Zelesz. The young Countess Karoline became somewhat more friendly, but the relationship always remained rather superficial. His mood was not improved. "How should we," he wrote, "begin to be happy; as unhappiness is the only charm that is left to us?" Each of his friends was in another corner of the world. How he yearned towards the former days when they were all confidentially together and each revealed the children of his art to the other, with parental shyness. Do we discern this nostalgia in the A Minor Quartette? He wrote a great deal for four hands at Zelesz. Duets are Schubert's simultaneous expression of the intimate and the social, and became an original art in his hands.

He lived with Bauernfeld a sort of communal existence. Lanner came closer: The "Waltz community" comes to mind. Franz Lachner, who had received the position of organist at the Protestant Church, joined them. As long as they sat there together, Schubert, Schwind and Lachner, they must have been in their element. But is it not unimportant to repeat this again and again? Once Lachner met Schubert and Lanner. Lanner had never known Lachner personally. Schubert introduced him. "Yes, yes, all Franzes have something

Lichtenthal, a suburb of Vienna where Schubert grew up

Antonio Salieri, Schubert's music teacher

Ferdinand, Schubert's oldest brother

to them." [1] It is not in the nature of a biography to write thus; but, generally speaking, there can be no biography of Schubert's life, in which the outer events were so sparse. About this time Milder wrote to him to ask if he could give her an opera for Berlin. He packed up "Alphonse and Estrella" again. After three months it was returned. She wrote: "If I'm to have the pleasure of appearing in one of your operas, it must be cast for my personality; for example the rôle of a queen, a mother, or a peasant. To this end I would advise you to create something new—say—an oriental plot in which I would be the central figure. This you would do well, as far as I can observe from Goethe's 'Divan' (Suleika). You could be sure of three people and the chorus for a good presentation here— namely, a soprano, a tenor and a bass. Should you find such material, I beg you advise me of it so that we can come to terms. At which time I'll use all means to get it produced." Schubert did not allow himself to be dictated to; he simply ignored the whole matter.

The journeys must have been very pleasant. As a rule Vogl took him along, even once to Gastein, where Vogl went because of his gout. At Gastein Schubert wrote a symphony that was mislaid in

[1] Bie implies that this sentence may hide a pun—which is untranslatable.

Vienna and has never been found. He went about as a guest, played here and there, and wrote charming letters about Salzburg. The piano sonatas show this epoch of his creativeness. Honorariums—somewhat better. Post as Court Organist—laid aside. That is, he resigned it. Better be independent. "The state should support me," he said, "so I may be untroubled and free to compose." Possibly, he did not wish to practise and take the examinations. What could that be for him?

He tried Goethe again. He dedicated some songs and sent them to him: "Your Excellency, if through the dedication of these settings of your poems I can prove my unbounded veneration of your Excellency and at the same time win some attention for my humble work, I shall prize such a success as the most beautiful experience of my life. With greatest respect, Your sincere servant Franz Schubert." Goethe made this note: "Message from Schubart from Vienna concerning my song-compositions."

So far, I have been faithful to the accuracy of Walter Dahms. Now I come to a place where he describes how, on this very same day, "Mendelssohn sent Goethe his three piano quartettes, and how Schubert suffered in comparison." Schubert, hindered by the reticence of the German worker, overthrown by the son of Abraham Mendelssohn, the Berlin banker! How is it possible to say such things? We should not shield Goethe in this instance. On the contrary, one ought to take him to task for it, without excuses. That is; the great author should not have utilized this opportunity to approach Father Abraham in this manner. How ugly it all is!

It is not my desire to write another "book" about Schubert, least of all as a musical scholar or a meticulous biographer. I let myself be carried by a light wind through the thorny woods of his life, through the rose-gardens of art, where I commune with his spirit. Did he really live? Do all these books carry more conviction than one of his waltzes? The philologicians say: "We can prove his life." But what is established? I could project another life for him, with Karoline von Esterhazy, in Hungarian castles, in the palaces of Vienna, through woods and fields, in radiance and delight, for seventy years; and still it would be far from the fact. I am too little the statistician. I have a horror of reading books in order to borrow biography from them. And how long did it take for his myth to descend from the spheres into the libraries? In the seventies Kreissle von Hellborn first tried to collect a few facts. He could never learn anything conclusive about the B Minor Symphony from the Hüttenbrenners. It was first discovered on May 1, 1865, by Herbeck, and produced in December. Anselm arranged it for four hands, and guarded it jealously. No one else knew of it, except his brother Joseph. Then for the first time there appeared the large complete edition, in which Breitkopf and Härtel atoned for the sins they had committed against Schubert. Much came to light for the first time, Mandyczewski wrote his careful notes—much still remains in oblivion. It is almost mythical that such an artist, wandering carelessly over the earth for a couple of decades, scattered his works, now here, now there, so carelessly that his disciples have been gathering them slowly—or seeking them vainly—ever since. Known to us only through echoes of his contemporaries, this life, which was scarcely lived, is too impalpable to be spread out in a biography! When I see all these books, then the writing of Heuberger, to whom some hitherto unknown details came by chance, the delightful little book of Klatte, the still incomplete documentary collection of Otto Erich Deutsch, the countless essays in Germany, France and England, the general opinion precipitated into letters for a poor lonely Viennese musician, my love for his ethereal work mounts far above all writings—and I cannot read them. Disturbed though I am at this one place in Dahms' book, I must confess there was much I never knew till I found it in these pages, and that I was startled to observe how much has been written and printed about this living-unliving spirit. It is the spirit that I would rescue, ignoring the material evidence, untroubled if a letter resounds thus or so, if the chronology is false or true, if the thoughts of the others occur here or there. It is not the body of the man I would reproduce, but the soul of his music—timeless, spaceless,—as he demands, who, although embedded in the world, overcame it.

It may happen that someone will read this book, and not merely run through it for the sake of the pictures. In that case, the foregoing protest will either exasperate him or move him to sympathy. If it impresses him unfavorably, may he forgive me that I have approached Schubert from a different angle than his other biographers. This method can never quite succeed, for we are spoiled. But it will never succeed better than with such a subject. And if the reader agrees with what I say, and meets me half way, I promise to liberate him sooner than another from the letter of the word, and leave him with the pictures. How often has the same thing happened to me! I did not sink myself in the illustrations from any distaste of reading, but rather from a sensual pleasure, the physical emotion through the medium of sight, through which the limited intellect was transfigured. Now

I can recognize Herr Schober in all his elegance, can see the imposing Vogl next to the self-effacing Schubert, and can visualize the way they walked and talked together. I thank the good Schwind most of all. With his eternal sketching (principally in the long account of Lachner's life) he caught the true Schubert characteristic and brought us a little nearer to his essence. Anselm Hüttenbrenner's sharp, sympathetic face remains unforgettable; and there remains something of the atmosphere in which these people arranged their simple, satisfied and so unpolitical lives. Yes, this lack of politics—how enviably it surrounded Schubert's problem-free music. What a hard time he had, although there is not a trace of it in his work. Beethoven tore agony out of himself; but anguish only established Schubert the more securely in his spiritual island. Do we know anything of his outward form? Can we guess, in spite of all the pictures, exactly how he looked, how he moved, how he spoke? Must we stick our noses into books again to experience (through the eyes of a leading veterinary) how it stood with him? Do we know whether this medico observed well and noted carefully? He describes him anatomically: the form small but well-set, strongly developed, firm bones and tight muscles, more rounded than angular. Do you wish to hear more of what Doctor Eckel says? An intensity that

[32]

charmed people with more than any facial expression or outward appearance. What was this appearance? Eckel reports: Neck short and strong; shoulders, breast and back broad and well-arched; arms and thighs rounded; hands and feet small; the tread lively and vigorous; the head rather large and crudely rounded, ringed with brown, luxuriantly growing curly hair. The face, in which the brow and chin were prominently developed (this hardly tallies with the pictures), showed features rather less beautiful than expressive. The mild and, if I am not mistaken, light-brown eye, which in excitement grew fiery, was deeply shadowed because of jutting arches and bushy brows; and frequent squinting (a habit of short-sighted persons) made it seem smaller than it really was. His nose, medium, stumpy, somewhat retroussé (this cannot be observed in the pictures) was bound by a gently concave curve to the full and tight-closing mouth below which we see the so-called "beauty-dimple" in his chin. His face was pale but lively as is the case with all geniuses. A quick play of feature expressed the constant inward excitement—sometimes in a deep frown or tightly closed lips, often in the soft light of the eye and the smiling mouth— foreshadowing the presence of his creative genius. In its entirety, Schubert's form was the classic combination of strength and mildness that one associates with the Olympians. (In such phrases one recognizes the level and worth of this description.)

Even now he is becoming unreal to us. Smiling compassionately, he looks down upon earth. "Soon, dear writer, your task will be ended," he thinks. "Why do you wish to relate so much? Yes, I remember, two years before my death everything was sad and desolate. All was over with the Esterhazys. My royalties were small. There was no response. Sickness weakened me. Have I not said that the deepest springs issue from pain? It was the time of the D Minor Quartette. There was never any question of a public performance. It was played privately here and there. And my friends? They married.

"My application for the position of Court Kapellmeister? 'Your Majesty! all-bountiful Kaiser! In deepest reverence the undersigned dares respectfully to request the granting of the vacant post of Second Kapellmeister and supports his attempt by citing the following reasons: (1) He was born in Vienna, the son of a schoolmaster, and is 29 years old; (2) He himself enjoyed your most high protection for five years as one of the Court Singers in the Imperial Convent; (3) He received complete instruction in composition from the then Court Kapellmeister Anton Salieri, by virtue of which he is fitted to fill any position as Kapellmeister—witness the enclosure (recommendation by Salieri); (4) His name is favorably known not only in Vienna, but throughout all Germany, because of his songs and instrumental compositions; (5) He has five masses ready to be played in various churches in Vienna, completely arranged for small and large orchestra; (6) He occupies no post, and hopes by this means to win security and reach his goal in art. He will never cease striving to come up to your highest expectations.

" 'Your humblest servant,

" 'FRANZ SCHUBERT

" 'Vienna, April 7, 1826.' "

. . . .

'All his efforts were unsuccessful. Equally unsuccessful was the appeal to Beethoven. We know that Beethoven said: "Truly, in Schubert dwells a godly spark." He said this when Schindler brought him a few songs for an opinion. Perhaps he might have asked to see some of the operas and symphonies, but death overtook him. Blackness triumphed in the only moment when Schubert was near. Did Schubert visit him as he lay dying? Did he see him for the first time only when he was dead? Was this the moment, when, for the first and last time, he entered his dwelling? Beethoven was lowered into the grave in the Währinger Cemetery. Schubert and his friends foregathered in the Mehlgrube (restaurant) on the Neuen Markt (New Market Place) and Schubert raised his glass: "To him whom we have just buried." Then he lifted the second glass: "To him who will be the next." A good legend.

Hoffmann von Fallersleben journeyed with Panofka to Dornbach to see Schubert. They inquired for him in the "Kaiserin von Oesterreich" (Empress of Austria). They were told: "He has not come to Dornbach for some time. Today is Saturday—perhaps he'll come tomorrow." The next morning they sought him again unsuccessfully. Then they wrote and invited him to "Der Weisse Wolf." Wine was placed on the table for him, but he did not come so they drank his wine and departed. Fourteen days later they celebrated Mariä Himmelfahrt (Mary's Ascension into Heaven). Together the two took the stage coach to Nussdorf. They searched for him all over Vienna, but could not find him; they trudged to Heiligenstadt and then to Grinzing, where they stopped. The wine was poor, but it was pleasant to sit in the garden; an old fiddler was playing. Suddenly Panofka called out "There he is." Surrounded by several young girls, he was looking for a seat. Panofka pulled him over. Hoffman von Fallersleben expressed his great joy. Schubert stood embarrassed before him, hardly knowing what to answer. After

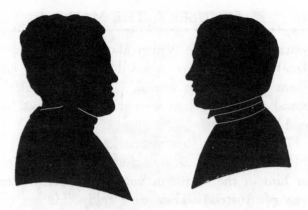

Schubert's stepbrothers, Andreas and Anton

Silhouette of Schubert in 1817

Municipal hospital, church and Karntnertor Theater, which Schubert as a boy visited frequently

a few words he excused himself and vanished for good. Fallersleben summed up the encounter with this banal remark: "I wish I had never seen him. Then I would not have known how commonplace and indifferent he was." So that incident is closed.

It is unnecessary to dwell on the rest of his life. Let us not count his visits and invitations, but rather his fatigue and despair. "Die Winterreise" (The Winter Journey) is the deepest expression of this gloom. He lived in the irony of the poet Müller. He said: "Soon you will hear and understand. Come today to Schober's and I'll sing you a series of shattering songs. They have gripped me as no other songs have done." This was also the period of the little piano pieces, in which he created the prototype of wordless lyrical expression for the instrument. Here we see the very lips moving.

And now that last year. Poor man! His stepmother guarded in a stocking the proceeds of the copy-books that his father sold in the school. The son visited her Sundays: "Now lady mother, let me look about a bit—perhaps you'll find a couple of twenties in your stocking that you could give me for a good afternoon." And she gave them. He loafed with Bauernfeld and Schwind. At nightfall they accompanied one another home, they took turns sleeping at one another's houses. Schwind lay in a leather coverlet on the floor. Hats, boots, cravats, coats—they shared them together. Schubert received his royalty—and that day they lived luxuriously.

As a final experience, there was the one concert that Schubert gave, on the 26th of March, 1828. Concert? There was a movement from a string-quartette; Vogl sang a couple of songs; Josephine Fröhlich sang the "Ständchen," with the female pupils of the Conservatory; there was a new trio; someone sang "Auf dem Strom" (On the River), by Rellstab, with horn and piano; Vogl sang the "Allmacht" (The Almighty), and, as a finale, the Battlesong for male voices. Schubert gave the concert at his own risk. It was crowded and the proceeds were good, nearly eight hundred guldens. Schubert was called out countless times but the critics killed him with silence. Dare he expect anything better? German publishers, for the first time, showed an interest of their own accord, but very little came of it. What came, from that little room, were the great C Major pieces, the Symphony, and the Quintette. Then death looked at him. Meals stood untouched. He moved from Schober to his brother Ferdinand. A requiem composed by Ferdinand was produced in the district church at Hernals. This was the last music Schubert heard. We may wonder whether it suggested to him his own approaching death. Nevertheless, he made his last journey to the theoretician Simon Sechter. It is pleasant to imagine that Schubert still wanted to learn theory and arrangement—perhaps for his choruses in heaven. On November 12th, he wrote to Schober: "I am ill—for eleven days I have eaten nothing and drunk nothing. I wander wearily, and wobble from chair to bed and back again. Send me reading matter, preferably J. Fenimore Cooper. Leave it in the coffee house with Frau von Bogner. My brother will fetch it—or anything else. . . ." November 19th was the end. According to the story he cried in agony: "It is not Beethoven who lies here!" For this reason he was laid next to Beethoven in the Währinger Cemetery, and later his corpse was interred with Beethoven's in the Central Cemetery.

The Court had to dispose of only his earthly estate. There were three dress-coats, three frock coats, ten pairs of trousers, nine vests, one hat, five pairs of shoes, two pairs of boots, four shirts, nine kerchiefs, thirteen pairs of socks, one sheet, two bed covers, one mattress, one bolster, one cover—altogether worth 53 guldens. His books, with the exception of a few old music books, valued at 10 guldens, were conspicuous by their absence.

As I write this, 1450 gold marks have been paid at an auction for one of Schubert's letters. *Sic crescit gloria mundi.*

PIANO MUSIC

I COME now to the works themselves. I shall not consider them in chronological order. It is possible, of course, to trace a development from the simple to the complicated, from the superficial to the profound, but I prefer to outline his system (the system of his entire work) from the musical picture he left us. Fate broke the thread of his life and work. To imagine how the latter may have developed, we need only to examine the elements which compose it. I shall not make a comprehensive survey; I shall examine only the things which the world knows—or should know. Let us begin with the smallest works, the piano pieces, and go on to those of a more complicated nature. No attempt will be made to supply erudite notes; I shall merely explain and appraise certain favorites and give reasons for their appeal.

As a first example, let us consider the four Impromptus (opus 90), those small pieces introduced into piano literature by Schubert. Beethoven's Bagatelles mark a preliminary state, being merely uncompleted sonata movements, sketches of an idea. Here is conscious completion. These small pieces might easily have been arranged into sonatas (romantic sonatas being composed of just such elements); but it is more enlightening not to arrange them so but to discuss them individually as one poem after another. We are never so near Schubert's soul as in these miniatures. There is no musical person to whom they are not familiar and beloved. A folk-tune is sounded, a song, but not the

IMPROMPTU, OPUS 90, I

1. Klavier Impromptu op. 90,1

Allegro molto moderato

common sort, one less carefree and more meditative. The piano takes it appreciatively. The melody is nakedly set forth, then clothed in simple chords. As with the first part, so with the second. The theme is repeated; the harmonies become richer and weightier. On a broken bass, from the same melody, there develops an extended

[41]

theme, which spreads over the keyboard. Having descended, in fluttering figures, the theme remounts from the bass and rests in a lulling A Flat Major. The poet returns to the first form of the folk-tune, decks it richly in triplets, sublimates it, tries it in sixteenths, caresses it with stretching fingers, draws the theme back into triplets, then further back into fourths, until it dissolves in a breath and ceases to exist.

The second Impromptu presents quite another picture, with its fleeting runs in E Flat Major, its staccato middle movement in B Minor, revolving with pianistic sensitivity suggestive of Chopin, as Schubert seldom is. His piano pieces, which sometimes retain traces of virtuosity, reach their most individual expression in cadences, in velvet harmonies and soft refractions, rather than in fortes forced to reveal a sudden impulse.

The third piece is wholly an expression of tenderness. It is said that Schubert conceived it still more ethereally in G Flat Major, but finally chose G Major to make it easier for the performer. A song, sung from the depths of his romantic soul, expands in infinite length and breadth above a broken accompaniment; sometimes against a counterpoint of the second theme played in the bass. The piece is the very measure of Schubert's gifts. With indescribable delicacy the fingers draw from

IMPROMPTU, OPUS 90, 3

2. Klavier Impromptu op. 90,3

the keyboard the breath of the soul itself. The
breast rises and falls with emotion.

The fourth piece has the character of a light
improvisation with a sharp change in the middle
passage. Schubert often chose this traditional
method when he wished to create an effect by contrast instead of by simplicity.

The other four Impromptus are, as a whole, in-
ferior. Nevertheless, the legato movement of the
second (A Flat Major) is unforgettable. One is always freshly surprised at the unexpected profusion
of his invention—a pre-Schumann romanticism
that flowers in the "Rosamund" variations. Let us
examine the final movement in the last, the F
Minor. The capricious beginning is negated by a
dull middle section. It is a relief to see that even
Schubert could have his weak movements. Otherwise the perfection of his genius would be almost
unbearable.

The "Moments Musicals" are six pieces of incredible variety. A C Major bursts from the strings
like a trumpet-blast. It is given contour and color
by happy chords. It broadens perceptibly, diminishes to the call of a cuckoo, and finally becomes
a figure uniting itself with the theme. Here is the
very play of Romanticism. Then, back to the beginning, to the trumpet call; since structure is
paramount. A motive in A Flat Major is punctu-

ated with fifths and sixths (fingers have been familiar with these intervals as late as Brahms) and shaded with an F Sharp Minor theme. Through it all, the delicate chords smoothly support the song, which is heard again, and which could be heard through eternity.

MOMENTS MUSICALS, NO. 3

3. Moments musicals Nr. 3

It has been played ten million times, this teasing whimsicality in F Minor, which flirts with F Major on those borders of major and minor over which Schubert liked to flit with such ease and humor. Now the C Sharp Minor phrase enters (an agitated study in sixteenths) interrupted by the

warm pianissimo of a syncopated A Flat movement. Then F Minor again, but this time a vigorous pacing in quarter and two eighth notes, lifted
up in a true Schubertian circling of keys.

MOMENTS MUSICALS, NO. 6

This could be called his Credo. A man sits at
the piano, lightly touches an A Major chord and
lets the drooping cadences fall through the related keys to E Major. This sensitivity is slightly
accented in a middle section, called the Trio. It is
transported as though it were in love with itself,
running parallel to the other voices that seem to be
joining it in a folk-song. The spirit of another age
is recaptured, as we return to the principal theme,
with which we can never become satiated.

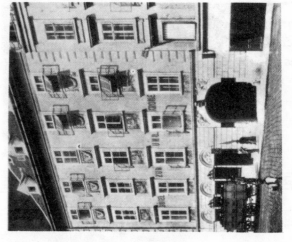

The Inn "Zur Ungarischen Krone" where the "Schubertianer" held meetings

Courtyard view of the school house in Säulengasse 3

Excursion of the "Schubertianer"

FANTASY IN G. MAJOR, OPUS 78

5. Fantasie G-Dur op. 78

Molto moderado e cantabile

That amazing Fantasy, Opus 78. Fantasy! Four movements are combined, each of which leads its own Schubertian life. Each could serve as a separate impromptu. The first is in A Major—nothing more than a variation of Schubert's favorite treatment of the piano: the far-spread, tender chords succeeding each other in new positions, new disguises, new and secret combinations. At first, the right hand guides a motion of three eighths on four sixths, which characterized, until Schumann, the noble rhythm of this genre. Schumann! After a brief, virtuoso episode, there occurs a descending passage, a melodic scaffold, a curious caressing figure which determined half of Schumann's literature. Development? A passing counterpoint, like a canon in the middle of the piece, might be so considered. But it does not concern Schubert for long. Only too willingly, he returns to the frank tone of the beginning. The second movement (Andante) interrupts a romantic folk-song by a wild outburst of quasi-Hungarian feeling, and this outburst subsides in a peaceful meditation in F Sharp Major. The third movement (Minuet) has the dance in its fingers. The Trio, in a grandiose B Major, contains a hint of Schubertian waltz, like a turning away from a more complicated time, in the very midst of great music, toward a half-forgotten naïveté. The fourth section also has national color.

(LAST MOVEMENT) FANTASY IN G. MAJOR, OPUS 78

Is this, likewise, somewhat Hungarian? Zelesz? Karoline? It passes between song and humming, fiddle-figures and a skipping dance; always joyfully and exuberantly. Suddenly we are moved by the touching *espressivo* in C Minor, changing abruptly to C Major, a charming piano device. And once more we return to the humming and dancing—and a light "Thank-you" at the end.

The well known "Wanderer" fantasy (Opus 15) is developed from the theme of the immortal song, especially in the middle movement, where the dark mood is condensed. But the Wanderer Fantasy is not gloomy, and the resemblance is only superficial. It is, by the grace of the piano, an individual work. There is, on the whole, not much more left of the theme *qua* theme than the Schubertian movement of the hand, so often employed by him in a succession of one quarter and two eighth notes. It would be false to call this program-music, reflecting the sentiments of the Wanderer: "Joy is always in the place where one doesn't happen to be." Quite the contrary. Joy is here; it exists in pure sensuousness. The theme is detached from the song, translated in sheer tone, reflecting joy in its unwavering treatment. If it were not for the accompanying sentiment, one might almost say that the treatment is artificial. Even if it were artificial, it is pleasant to see Schubert sitting at the piano, freeing himself from his visions in the mood of the moment, always finding a way back to his spiritual self, apart from mere sensation. Is it possible to accept a descriptive expanding of a theme

[49]

from a delicate concept into a powerful pianistic effect, transfigured by numberless variations? It is possible, because of the purity of an art which Schubert never loses. One cannot accept it when Liszt makes an arrangement of the same piece— an arrangement that debases the spirit of the original, and, with specious rhetoric and false brilliance, turns it into the semblance of a concert with orchestra.

The rhythmical theme breaks through with a broad chord in C Major; the fingers exult in the firm attack, strongly supported in firm sequences, and are whirled down till the motive in E Major begins to breathe softly with gradual change. This changing becomes more independent; the voices are drawn singing over the keys; the masculine C Major ascends to the heights, and the imitative play begins in all parts of the theme, quieting itself in E Flat Major, closing lyrically, with continually new changes, in a play of fantasy. The rhythms grow greater and stronger, storming over the piano. Gradually, with decreased quivering, they reach C Sharp Minor, and descend to the source of inspiration, to the wander-theme itself, quite pianissimo— quite sunk in itself.

Variations play. The theme is sung, with infinite tenderness and delicate changes, through E Major,

a whirlpool in the bass, a rolling up to the thirty-
seconds. The theme mysteriously returns to its line,
decorates it above heavy chords, sings itself free
into C Sharp Major, develops into an intricate C
Sharp Minor, returns heavily to C Sharp Major,
and at last resolves in an ethereal play of sixty-
fourths that rush, crying wilder in sevenths, and
give the effect of an almost toneless tremolo—the
dark background on which the silver motive still

WANDERER FANTASY IN C MAJOR, OPUS 15
7. Wandererfantasie C=Dur op. 15

glistens—and suddenly the Presto seizes us. The
motive exists only as an illusion of a Scherzo. It
dances, springs, masks itself, and suddenly jumps
into D Flat Major and creates a little song, perhaps

[51]

from this closing cadence—perhaps from somewhere else. But the song is lovely, and sings in our ears like a secret waltz. It is the trio. The first section *da capo*. Transitions? There are no pauses between the phrases. The whole is one long phrase. It contains the different tempi, the different figures, and leads one into the other. Was it this that stimulated Liszt? His symphonic poems were nothing more than the carrying out of this method. The Wanderer Fantasy was the first symphonic poem for the piano. And the program? If one wants to adhere to it, the slow passage belongs to the mood of the Wanderer. But perhaps it is somewhat too dæmonic for that. The surge of the first phrase, the happiness of the third; these are the usual properties that we find in every symphony. And so it is with the working out of the last theme. The theme becomes a fugue. The fugue is security, harbor, and quiet after storm. Themes of the first part are contained in it; the musical experience is over; the piano triumphs in a victorious breadth, in the sun of C Major.

Many sonatas remain. They are not equally important. I underline some and select the beauties of others: I write as an amateur about the things he loves, not as scholar about details that he has discovered. I am wary of literary affectations. How easy it would be to make poems about music.

But it would be false to confuse one art in terms of another—and never express either. Besides, it would be unmusical. Music has a store of definite technicalities which the reader need not fear. Even without an understanding of these, he recognizes the contrasts made by major and minor, and he will always take pleasure in Schubert's use of these contrasts. Perhaps he already knows something of the character of the different keys; what one gains by calling pieces or sections by their particular signatures. He will perceive A Minor is a favorite key of Schubert, because it moves so easily and innocently. He will realize the same of A Flat Major, G Flat Major and D Flat Major, because they seem to be the keys in which tenderness is most fluently expressed. And if he once sees that the tonic is the basic tone, the dominant the leading, and that the interval of the seventh holds the power of greatest suspension, he will be able to construe all the other musical relations, and will be prepared for the vast varieties of harmony—from a base that implies the sixth position (in itself a floating expectation) and from the chord of the sixth-fourth which expresses the whole longing towards finality—and the cadence.

All this had to be said. It is necessary to establish a complete understanding, a Schubertian understanding, with scholarly insight but emotional

[53]

appreciation—a necessary and intimate relation between the work and the listener.

But I wanted to speak of the sonatas. My favorites are neither the earliest nor the latest, but the beloved A Minor and still more famous D Major of his middle period.

There is such an ease of invention for the keyboard in the A Minor Sonata that it might be said that one who hears it walks in music. The themes and their dexterous development are never the most important with Schubert, rather a sense of the love and generosity which offer themselves to us, and the depth out of which they smile. The A Minor begins like a folk-dance; then it grasps the chords, leaps over the figures, caresses the themes, lets them jump and dance, even does them the honor to be treated in a scholarly fashion, or to be placed in a well-meant canon. But this is only the appearance; these are but the forms of pleasure, the joy in modulated harmonies and rhythms. The slow movement relies a little on the old scheme of variations. But this is much less important than the marvellous wealth of inspiration that blooms, on this occasion, from the keys, in a strength and variety foreshadowing the symphonic Etudes of Schumann. But the most charming is still the Scherzo, with its lively, swinging time, indescribably vigorous, almost bursting with inventiveness.

Or is the last movement the triumph? This rapid sea of eighths, the sudden glance from the waves, first here, now there, then in still another surge of keys. And among Schubert's exulting fourths and eighths and the tramping of forte harmonies, one after another, four times G Major and then four times E Major, four times C Major, four times A Major—and, under it all, over the ride of the eighth notes, the breath of a melody—never to be exhausted.

That was the A Minor, Opus 42. But there are other A Minors. The D Major Sonata is Opus 53. It has a greater sweep, it is more elemental; in the case of Schubert, broader, higher, deeper. The first movement rolls and hammers over the keyboard in an unconventional arrangement of chords and triplets. New figures appear; one feels courage and inspiration. The soul of a violin is counterpoised. There are inserted parts, in a retarded tempo, in which arpeggios of the Viennese fiddle paint figures for no other reason than that they are lovely and add a new grace. It rolls on. Search out the first theme, search out the second. You will hardly recognize them in the flood of passion. But be quiet. The slow movement begins *con moto*. It is one of the holiest melodies that Schubert sang, with a part for the middle voices that recalls the very last of the romantic period.

[55]

SONATA FOR PIANO, OPUS 53

Wonderful! And this is only the beginning. It broadens. It feels its way through the softest parts of the instrument to be mysteriously sounded. The line is prolonged, as only Schubert could prolong it, into the most nostalgic line in German music. Characteristic little changes occur from above, from below, over the caressing tone; and there emerges a song so pure that the pianoforte is astonished at its unimagined possibilities. Like a folksong, in sixths, fifths, and thirds, a second theme twines itself through the related keys; the left hand takes it, outlines it, shades it, as if it were an improvisation of the fingers that do not want to touch the keys more than is necessary to bring out the subtlest implication. How the structure rises! What curious syncopation! The measure grows bashful. It draws back. Then it resumes its beat as the melody describes a new circle, a mystical tenderness. The mild air moves softly, in an illusion of song, whispered from lip to lip. The captivating modulations are a hint of communication. It is as though all schools and traditions were transcended by his felicity of repetition and decorations, a felicity that scarcely allows one to perceive its method. The melody repeats and varies itself, becomes richer and fuller, more embracing, and loses itself in a whispered descent.

The Scherzo is a joyful madness. Flowery waltz movements, punctuated with three-fourths notes; the great urge of the dance. The tenderness of the broadly suspended Schubert harmonies are inserted as middle movements. In the last Rondo, however, there is a playful cadence, not quite unified, as if one had overtired oneself. Springing figures, on a pounding bass, loosely multiplied; when they return, they are interrupted by playful exercises in winged, fugitive melodies. A hush—and they are gone.

These two exquisite sonatas date from 1825. The A Major, Opus 120, also belongs to this year. What a broad, singing theme stands at the beginning. And yet it does not fulfill all that the theme promises. It is extremely skilful, but sometimes a little empty. The fragment of the C Major (also of the same year), usually called the "Relic," is much more interesting. It stimulated a modern composer, Ernst Krenek, to finish it, which he did with genuine taste and discretion.

Schubert's sonatas were always born of sudden eruptions. In 1817 he wrote three. Naturally the early ones are simpler and milder. The most interesting is the A Minor Sonata, Opus 164. It has a charming second movement that deserves devotion. The theme is as joyful as a walking song. It is charmingly transposed and interrupted by pretty asides. The rondo-like transpositions show all the charm of Schubert's "line."

Then there are three sonatas which belong to the year 1828. The one in C Minor has an Adagio that flatters our ears by the softness of its melody, by the ripe flowering of its speech, by the color of its harmonic changes. In the final section of the same sonata, there is a tarantella-like movement in jumping fingers over the whole keyboard. Then there is a sonata in A Major, also remarkable for its structure and the sudden peculiarities native to

[58]

Atzenbrugg mansion where Schubert and his friends spent many happy hours

Frolic on the Atzenbrugg grounds

Schubert. It has an Andantino of a melancholy contour, drawn out of free figures and self-satisfying improvisations; it contains a Rondo, so full of singing strength that we see, rising from the keys, joyous brotherhoods which, in continual variations, continually recall their vows. How happily Schubert employed these bright themes. The B Minor Sonata develops from such a melody, now pianissimo, mystically; now forte, rejoicing aloud. An inexhaustible cornucopia shakes out endless new melodies, scarcely to be considered as themes. Once more we linger at the last movement of this sonata: A trumpet blast sounds a G, and from C Minor a light and endearing motive finds its way back to B Major, soon curving in a second theme of Hungarian character, in a third which suggests Schumann and a fourth, which whirls in southern passion. All are drawn into a welcome relationship, and a brilliant Presto closes the concert.

Now we approach a new kind of loveliness. I will spin no long phrases; I will not exaggeratè; I will speak just as Schubert composed, simply and intimately. But if something pleases, I will repeat it and spin out the thread as long as seems desirable. I speak of his dances for the Piano; first of all of the Waltzes, which established one of the gayest

[59]

regions in the history of music. They sprang from the people. Art had already heard them, but from a distance. One catches glimpses of them, somewhat shamefaced, in the old symphonies, in the trios of Scherzi, but they are hidden; the Viennese waltz was not yet recognized by the Muse. Schubert did not hesitate. The Ländler and waltzes dropped like pearls from his fingers. He discovered them in quantities and wrote them down in long lines, sometimes helter-skelter, sometimes bound together by a mood. What he intuitively discovered

WALTZ FOR THE PIANO, OPUS 9, VOLUME 2, NO. 14

9. Klavier Walzer op. 9 Heft 2 Nr. 14

became the fashion of his time: the domination of pure melody. Lanner continued this tradition; so did the Johann Strausses, father and son; it be came one of the most pleasurable occupations of the world. For the first time, music of the dance was admitted into the temple without reservations.

The unbelievable happened. To conduct a melody over lightly moving harmonies in three-fourths time became not only an act of imagination but also a triumph of craftsmanship. Love of song joined the love of the dance. Schubert expressed an endless variety of moods by the simple device of developing a natural and fluent melody, based on the most rudimentary musical laws, and proceeding from direct inspiration. These new creations attain inexhaustible charm and rejuvenation by being held in a rhythm that has never ceased to delight. The motive power of this invention found expression in maintaining a unity of contrast: melody set against rhythm and harmony. Schubert exhausted every possibility of these charming devices. He perceived and expressed, throughout its entire range, the flowering æsthetic of the Viennese waltz.

I have played them a thousand times, written about them almost as many. In the whole field of music, nothing lies so close to me as these distinctive simplicities. They are as fresh as the day I first discovered them. My tattered copy of Schubert Dances is a witness to my love. For decades it has stood on the music-rack and has with-

[61]

stood every assault. Many of the dances which are particularly happy have been underscored in blue, and some of these which seem especial proof of his genius I have again underscored in red. Only yesterday I played them all through and found some I had forgotten, and I know I shall forget many which I have newly found. And I will keep on returning to this source, as though I had never been there, and I shall always be refreshed.

Can anyone describe the variety with which Schubert's imagination developed the problem of drawing a melodic line above a rhythmic harmony? Sad or nostalgic waltzes—to whom do the melodies belong, to whom can Science attribute them? How much has come from the people, how much from the air, from the climate, singing itself into his ear in order to find expression through the piano? The natural way to swing the waltz into full motion is to proceed from the tonic. But Schubert has an unusually beautiful method. The movement is casual at first; the stream of melody is uncertain, as though not sure of its direction; it wanders through related keys till it determines upon its own. It is impossible to estimate how often Schubert's preamble has been copied. His is so suave and amiable a method of introducing the waltz that it has captivated all his successors. One sees, for example, that instead of beginning on the tonic, he starts on a dominant seventh, drops to the fifth below, where the entire waltz remains floating in the air until, just at the close, it sinks happily into the tonic. It is an endless pleasure to perceive the charm with which the development of a melodic phrase is consummated in a series of changing harmonies. The phrase is stated; its form remains the same. But its manner is changed, with its position in D Flat Major, in A Flat Major, or in E Flat Major; and this metamorphosis is accomplished with such compelling grace that the piano itself seems to dance.

WALTZ FOR PIANO, OPUS 9, VOLUME I, NO. 6

One would like to copy the melodies graphically as they occur, in varied rhythms, merely changing the living picture of double three-fourths time into new guises, each bearing the same freshening word.

The movement, cajoled from top to bottom in short figures, regains the heights in one long ornate figuration. Or a pianissimo phrase suggests the fillip of a *sforzato*. Or, with a long breath like a slow song, the melody stretches itself to the breaking-point. Or teasing remonstrances from below induce a tender mood. Broken chords skip with trills. The first strong beat of the time draws the melody like a train behind it. Fine harmonic surprises leap suddenly from F Major to D Flat Major, then sink into the tonic with that sweet submission which was Schubert's chief harmonic virtue. But the three-fourths time acts only as accompaniment, as chords—1 2 3 4 5 6—returning to 1 in order to paint a graceful ascending melody that expresses its contentment in sixths. Wide stretches; ringing chords; soft parallel Schubert fingers play with the three-fourths time in an extraordinarily personal way. Lights twinkle in an endless perspective of Ländler.

His aims grow greater. The tension expands in a wide circle. The keys remember their mission. The waltz rises in a higher and more imaginative structure, beginning in a courageous E Major of resounding chords. A melody in an ennobled waltz style, a model for Schumann, strains over the bars, creating a contrast. These delicate constructions are almost impromptus that develop lyrically and dramatically in three-fourths time. Again there are flowing scales, sharpened themes of almost Mazurka character. A midday sun illumes the landscape. Ländler go by, shouting. It was Opus 18, No. 1; now it is No. 2. Endless joy, twitter of larks, whisper of trees, swaying of grass-blades, blessedness of Nature, fragrance of fields, untouched nobility of meadows.

VALSES SENTIMENTALES, OPUS 50, VOLUME 1, NO. 13

11. Valses sentimentales op. 50 Heft 1 Nr. 13

In the German dances strength comes into the fingers, ingenuity into the spirit. The changes in the sections are sharper. Aspiration, love, playfulness, dance, longing, levity, day-dreaming in the dominant, modulated in minor, and resolved in the tonic with a sad smile. Schubert's multi-colored voices are woven into an unbelievable tapestry of sound.

Among these sentimental waltzes, there is one in D Major where the left hand does not execute the usual swinging motion, but lightly alters its chords in order to follow the delicate line of waltz melody most gracefully, finding a golden mean between a song and a shout. Suddenly (*vide* No. 13) the left hand begins a simple A Major accompaniment, and in the second bar a melody is announced (the direction is "tenderly") which has become one of the most famous in a harsh and brutal world. No one can withstand it. It is composed of a phrase of four eighth-notes, a half-note and a quarter-note. But the melodic line is drawn over and under the harmonies with such potency that no greater Schubert, even in his largest works, can be imagined. And it is entirely Schubert in the way that the second part goes from A Major to C Sharp Major, and lets this same melody draw a deep breath in secret imitation of the first part, in order to restore it, as only he can do, with a slight gesture, to the original key.

There are endless changes. "Viennese Ladies Ländler": hesitate on the first beat; dance on the second and third; developing, broadening; and the untiring play of the small figurations goes on in their masquerade between dainty rococo and sentimental Biedermeier. "Valses Nobles": grandeur of carriage; large hewn figures; tense chords; the right hand in long-drawn-out six-eighths melodies; octaves, strong fingers, vigorous dance-tunes, rustic well-being; and, in between, a light dallying, as of the picking of a guitar, and a soupçon of sadness.

What did Liszt do? He picked these blossoms, and with them he decorated his "Soirées de Vienne." The flowers died. They had stood in God's free air, knowing nothing of the triumphs of a virtuoso. Painted and enamelled, these country flowers were placed before a public which, in the brilliance of the concert hall, was supposed to forget their origin. For God's sake! Keep your hands off such "adaptations" that betray Nature! Those who cannot understand such an art in its purity cannot understand it at all.

—Hitherto I could entertain myself at the piano alone. Now the ensemble begins. I lose myself in the Schubert ensemble. The duets demand a coupling. You must join me. Will you take the right or the left hand?

—Whatever you say.

—Very well, then, I'll take the right hand, to keep the lead. Schubert's music is better observed from this position. With Beethoven the opposite is true. Here melody is all. Even the harmony imagines itself a melody, a true sign of the Romantic.

FANTAISIE FOR FOUR HANDS, OPUS 103.

12. Fantaisie vierhändig op. 103

Allegro molto moderato

. . . But let us begin. Even while playing we can continue our observations. Well, sit down. The F Minor Fantasy. You begin. A lovely theme, isn't it, with the dotted rhythms that he loved. Splendid the way the harmonies shift.

—Now *I* have the melody. I believe we have divided the task equally.

—Notice how both voices are independently

[69]

treated. Accompaniment and melody are now above, now below; it is a true ensemble as of two instruments. Lovely the way one overlaps the other. Now D Major.

—Now minor again. I have a new theme. It mounts. It crosses over to you.

—Now I have it. We sing it together. How sweetly it distributes itself in the many voices which we are allowed to govern. Look out! Now we are at the beginning again and once more the second motive, but in major. And now, watch out: crescendo, F Major; suddenly F Sharp Minor. The Largo begins.

—We work in a canon; first you, then I, in these fine, strong attacks, and now in this singing melody. Suggestion of the cornet, eh?

—That is true. But still it is genuine. It *sounds*. Quiet yourself; we are again in the vigorous marked passages. *Allegro vivace*. Quicker! Ah, that's lovely! It plays itself. It rocks and balances and hurries on.

—The trio sounds almost Chopinesque—light, delicate.

—And the main portion again, so like Schumann. Stop! Tempo I. First theme again. Now major, now minor. Notice the large fugato on the second theme. Lovely, isn't it, how the theme

Inn "Zum Roten Igel," headquarters of the Society of the Friends of Music

Schubert's guitar

Pencil sketch of Schubert, by Kupelwieser, 1821

stretches, builds up, reverses, harmonizes itself. We are at the beginning again—and we are at the end.

—Now, shall we play the C Major Sonata? I remember Joachim once instrumented it. It is like a symphony.

—Yes. If you listen closely, you can almost distinguish the instruments. How greatly it is conceived. How comprehensive its architecture. Let us begin *moderato*. Fine, don't you think, this sudden pianissimo in E Major. Good, these thirds, always progressing, always quicker, E and C. Suddenly C Sharp Minor. We simulate an orchestra. Do you hear the clarinet? Now you have the second motive in A Flat.

—I play the 'cello. Now take it on the violin.

—I play all the instruments. Romantic! Wagner popularized this suspension. We are reminded of Weber now. All the great masters appear before us. Do you hear the rhythm of Weber? Do you hear the imitation of Schumann? For once, let's not talk. Let us enjoy the imaginative elaboration. . . .

—Ending in thirds. Suspended cadence. Indeed, quite Weber.

—We'll play the Andante without much reflection. It is so individual in melody, so graceful, not quite rococo, but still ornamented with bows and

[71]

ribbons. And these expirations! There is nothing more to say.

—It gives me pleasure to support the Scherzo with the thrusting bass, with *sforzati*, and to hear how you carry the *marcato*, changing its character in the treble.

—Attention. The Trio. The most mysterious of Schubert's pieces. More gently, more legato! Half creeping, half dragging. Always syncopate the bass notes between the melody and the middle-voice.

—Let us regale ourselves with the Vivace. It is not easy.

—Only listen how the melody skips and laughs, and accompany me whole-heartedly, gracefully. The Vivace always returns to the theme. Meanwhile we storm and subside—and take up the thread again. Now you, too, shall have your part of it. Now, both of us. Briskly onward, through the cycle of all the keys. Quicker! Keep time. A final laughter in C Major. Two triplets and two halves. Only in C. Finis. Thank you.

—What now? Shall we play all four volumes?

—Let us choose. The Variations, Opus 10, which he brought to Beethoven—oh, we can read them. Also those in A Flat Major. The Sonata in B, the Overture in F, the Rondo in A. It is merely a choice among many beauties. But don't let's distract ourselves. We'll take the loveliest. Open the book to Opus 144, that most characteristic Allegro which the publishers called "Life's Storms." It is short. Here is the first vigorous theme, and the second lyrical one. I never tire of it. It has a breath that only Schubert's melodies possess.

—Also this choral-like theme sounds marvellous. Soon it will be transposed in figurations. And there rises a motive. Of what does it remind you?

—I think of Barak in "Die Frau ohne Schatten." Strauss must have given him this archaic costume on purpose.

—Now we'll try the Hungarian divertissement. How often I played it as a child. How this first swinging Andante loses itself in the harmonies. And then this fortissimo and tremolo. They were my first naturalistic impressions. And these Hungarian finales here in E Flat Major. Always the repetitions of the rhythm, running through every key, and the echoing accompaniment and the rhapsodic strides. How pleasant to land back in Tempo I. And this lovely descent in sixths. All childhood rises before me. I have not played it for so long. Today I understand the sudden *fortes* and *pianos* much better, and the national major cadence. And now the march. Again with new and yet similar

13. Lebensstürme vierhändig op. 144

themes. They have accompanied me through life. Once the last movement was very difficult, with its marked attack and the pace and the harmonies which exhaust the piano in a great crescendo. It affects me even today, this infinite abundance of march and song motives, this unbelievably passionate rhythm of syncopated harmonies, this intoxication of keys, and the unbridled play of musical figures. True, it is a popular piece. But it remains immortal.

—Now that you've had your pleasure, let me have mine. Do you know what I propose? We'll run through all the stirring marches that he wrote for four hands.

—Not all. There are a couple so exquisite that if you don't mind, we'll repeat them once or twice.

—I agree heartily. Besides, one shouldn't try to absorb too much Schubert at one time. We are not writing a book. We are filling ourselves with his spirit. Begin here; the March in G Minor. Always *staccato*. Quite dryly, and then joy springs up, the more vividly by contrast. Lord, how beautiful! Can I ever describe it? I can only play it. Of course, let us play all the "repeats"; we can never have enough of them. Are these still marches? They are piano pieces which he never surpassed. How that sounds! This personal magic of the duets, these

MARCHES FOR FOUR HANDS, OPUS 40, NO. 2, TRIO

14. Märsche vierhändig op. 40 Nr. 2, Trio

tonal surprises! The Trio in G Major. Is there anything lovelier? Yes, there is the next march, in D Major, and the Trio in B Major, which is even more beautiful. How it plays and sings in a hundred happy voices! You, Schubert, you poor little nobody, you wrote all this! And what was your reward? Let us go on playing. There is so much novelty in these marches, such freshening of rhythms and folk-melodies in the trios, that one can never be sated. We have already played three hours. We can't find a better ending than here with the first of the so-called "Marches Militaires." It is one of the most famous pieces in world-literature, and a thousand fingers have worked over it. Children and greybeards play it.

—I forget everything.

—Forget everything. Turn back to the beginning. A short marking of time, then a phrase of melody. Genius has given it place and permanence. Play quietly and rather thoughtfully, for it is a simple piece, and many hearts have beat in time to it.

—And it is a march.

—And a true march. It soars and lifts the life which, in the trio, is reflected in the light play of the senses, and which returns to the rhythm of the first part with new ardor.

—Again.

—Yes—and again.

MARCHES FOR FOUR HANDS, OPUS 51, NO. 1

15. Märſche vierhändig op. 51 Nr. 1

Allegro vivace

SONGS

OUR ensemble is expanded; the voice is added to the piano, and poetry to music. The "lied" is created, the "lied" which proved to be the source of Schubert's greatest fame, even during his lifetime. There already existed the songs of Reichardt, expressing many moods, and those of von Zumsteeg with their lyric grace. But these were still confined within the bounds of the rationalistic style of classical writing, which gave attention to perfection of form rather than to accuracy of details. Schubert's "lied" stands on that strange frontier between form and content, between pictorial representation and melodic expression. From this point it expands in an infinite variety of musical expression, which, both as an intimate picture of an insignificant episode and as an intimate communication between words and sounds, has no equal. This came to be the most German of musical song-forms. Though Schubert initiated it, his work already contains all the various possibilities implicit in the form. He understood every kind of compromise that could be established between the text and the music, between the voice and the piano. The vernal fragrance of the German song hovers over his work. Thus he has won his way into the hearts of the people with a completeness granted to few musicians and to few works.

The mass of his work is stupendous. He wrote about 600 songs. Occasionally, as in the year 1815, when 150 songs were composed, this productivity is uncanny. Once he wrote eight pieces in one day. But he often changed the version a number of times till he himself, or the public, was satisfied with it. He was not always very discriminating in his choice of texts; eighty-five poets supplied him with words. He preferred Goethe and composed music to seventy-two of his poems. Schiller contributed forty-six poems, and Schubert's friend, Mayrhofer, no less than forty-seven. Which shall we choose? There is scarcely a single song to which we are wholly indifferent, because it is by him. Let us take them in groups, and choose therefrom what is peculiarly characteristic of his style. First there are the two groups of Müller Lieder; then come a number of the compositions on poems by Goethe; and finally, from the remainder, we will take whatever rises above the average. In the general practice of concert program-making, the same songs are repeated again and again. Sometimes a singer has the courage to give us an unknown song of Schubert, and we are astonished by its beauty; there is a wealth of delight still undiscovered in this mass of musical production. But on the other hand repeated public performance puts a certain popular stamp on the song. I am referring here above all to the evenings given by Arthur Schnabel and his wife. The performance of a song becomes pure joy when it emanates from two individuals who are moved by the music as if they were but a single soul. Schnabel's clear romanticism and limpid conception, joined to the heartfelt warm tone denoting the inner emotion of the singer, his wife, Therese, create a unified artistic whole, a complete reincarnation, which combines the tradition of the past with the tone of the present. In such moments Schubert lives more intensively than in any book. Then he really lives.

Wilhelm Müller was a Professor, of sorts, at Dessau. He wrote poetry, with indifferent success. Alluding somewhat mysteriously to his own name, he wrote a cycle of harmless, simple poems, about the miller's beautiful daughter, simultaneously loved by a miller and a hunter. The miller throws himself into the mill-race when his rival prevails. The passion expressed is artificial, as is the structure of the inner conflict, more especially in its contrast of the colors, white and green; it smacked of the study. But in the movement of the whole poem, the

A game of charades. *Water color by Kupelwieser, 1821*

Esterhazy mansion in Zelesz, Hungary

Michael Vogl. *Lithograph by Kriehuber, 1830*

parallel drawn between the wanderlust and the onward rush of the water, in the play of alternating moods and the changing properties of nature and of music, lay distinct stimuli to musical composition. Schubert found the volume by accident on the table of a friend whom he was visiting, became absorbed in it, took the book along and began to work. He omitted several poems and composed the remainder as a cycle of separate songs, "An die ferne Geliebte." We shall find it expressive not interrelated musically as in Beethoven's cycle of his different styles, let us therefore try it.

16. THE MILLER'S BEAUTIFUL DAUGHTER
NO. 1. WANDERING

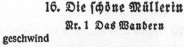

Mäßig geschwind

"To wander is the miller's joy." The poet gives us, in five verses, similes, parallel in construction, of the water, of the mill-wheels, of the mill-stones. He is anxious to make a wanderer of his miller. The composer's task is simpler. He writes the same folk-melody for all five verses, a popular tune which might have originated anywhere in the country, with sweet sudden cadences when he repeats the word "wandern"; to the piano he gives the rhythm of the miller's movements in swinging sixteenths. This makes a beautiful introduction.

He hears the brook gurgling and represents this with a melody which has all the easy flow of Schubertian imagination, glides easily through all the harmonies, finds new shapes with every new turn, yet still retains the perfection of structure. The lively part for the voice has a contrasted, rather formal piano accompaniment. The voice of the brook is given in rocking triplets, gurgling, rising and falling, chattering along, without end. The mill appears first in the piano, with a phrase that turns like one of its own wings. Gradually the voice is introduced welcoming the mill in a particularly sweet and peaceful manner. Schubert enters into every detail of the picture; the frame remains firm, only the drawing is changed. In gleaming contours the voice depicts shining windows, brilliant sunlight, sky. The piano answers smilingly, tenderly sounding the graceful chromatic transitions with which Schubert loves to color his melodic line. Was it so intended? "Was it so intended" are the first words of "Dankgesang" (Hymn of Thanks). The piano gets busier. It belabors a phrase which seems to turn on its own axis. The atmosphere is less cloudy while the piano plays a prelude. There are chords, runs, then the voice shapes contented melodies in an ordered calm. Now we have the peace of the evening and retrospec-

[85]

tion. The music is differentiated. The master miller speaks to the accompaniment of heavy chords, almost in recitative; the structure seems to be dissolved into sounds that are borne along by the vanishing day. Though formality tries to prevail, the voice is triumphant in a solo, singing dreamily and contemplatively, with the piano faithfully following its lead; thus a small epic of mood has been created. Now Schubert's workmanship grows more skilful. The "Neugierige" (The Curious One) seems to begin like a simple song, graceful of introduction, soulful in melody; but already in the middle part, where the rhythm is changed and the melody expanded, when the words "yes and no" are the import of the text, a long breath is taken and, freed from all rules, voice and hand reach out in broad parallel chords following only the inspiration of the moment. The beginning is not repeated nor does the frame of the picture matter when the changed measure gives entire liberty to the heart's need of expression.

In this song the height of Schubert's creative power is reached. "Ungeduld" (Impatience) is a masterpiece of invention and structure. Schubert again repeats the verses, with the same melody; but the manner in which he has conceived and constructed this song has been the model for hundreds of musicians. Fast triplets on the piano,

17. THE MILLER'S BEAUTIFUL DAUGHTER NO. 7, IMPATIENCE

rhythmically irregular, crowd together to form chords, leaving the voice free, allowing the melody to stream forth accentuated with light beats. Here is perfect romantic line which rises and falls with the emotion, in an indescribable euphony of leading, until with the "Dein ist mein Herz" the phrase itself is transfigured into an eternal expression, borne higher and higher with its own passionate force, till it descends, expiring quickly and bravely, in a graceful, satisfying cadence. Everything has been turned into sound. The words are ashamed of their limited powers. The voice carries the piano along with it, and the piano trembles with the voice. We have a rushing current of musical emotion whose inspiration is a divinity hitherto unknown to us.

[87]

Now there is an end of traditional structure. The future opens its gates, the heart has triumphed. All the rules which constrained emotion have lost their power. The song becomes conscious of its mission. It now possesses a thousand, nay a hundred thousand possibilities of intimate dramatic expression, of construction of emotional portrayal based on one rhythm, on one melody, no less than the possibilities of expressing a variety of feelings by different rhythms and melodies. They may be epical, lyrical, dramatic—all within the confines of a small space, as occasion requires—provided they are created by a soul filled with truth reacting in music to the impulse given by the poem. And you, my good Wilhelm Müller, you scarcely know how little you contributed to bringing about this transformation. You analyzed your feelings in neat categories, into the bark of the linden trees, young starlings, morning winds, and what not; but Schubert, reaching beyond your words, drew them into a living unit with the mighty breath of his music, and carried them to those eternal regions of which you had scarcely an inkling.

Wherever it is feasible, and even where it is not, Schubert makes use of this repetition of verses. This is really not a systematic treatment. In "Ungeduld" (Impatience) it actually impairs the rush-

ing flow of the melody to have it repeated four
times; but, nevertheless, the same feeling occurs
in every verse, always with slight variations. In
the "Morgengruss" (Morning Greeting) he might
easily have given us the four verses composed dif-
ferently one after the other; a new mood would
have been given in each one. But he preferred to
repeat the simple tune. The same thing might be
said of the "Müllers Blumen" (The Miller's Flowers). Though the content shows a progressive action, he is not disturbed by that but retains the
beautiful tune, four times in succession, and, at
the close, harmonizes the cadence in a most graceful way, first in straight then in curved lines, on
the refrain. In the "Tränenregen" (The Rain of
Tears) we have partly this, partly the other
method. The melody, like that of one of the early
nocturnes, unfolds gently, stretching over two
verses, interrupted by the chatter of the piano.
But in the fourth verse, at the words "my eyes
filled with tears, the mirror was clouded, she said,
'the rain is coming, farewell, I am going home,'"
the tune dutifully turns to sadness and is transposed to the minor key, modestly remembering
the major, but regains the minor with the dexterity
of Schubert's passage from one key to the other.

18. THE MILLER'S BEAUTIFUL DAUGHTER NO. 11, MY OWN

18. Die schöne Müllerin
Nr. 11 Mein

Mäßig geschwind

Bäch = lein, laß dein Rau = schen sein

Rä = der stellt eur Bräu = sen ein

Here we have an exquisite piece, portraying not only a climax in the young miller's emotions but showing no less what heights the invention of the composer could attain. He writes it with the rising and falling curve of life itself. But according to Schubert's judgment the eagerness of the young fellow was much greater than the joy of possession. Though he has at last won his sweetheart, he is musical enough not to use passionately crowded measures to proclaim his victory; in moderate fast time he begins on the piano with a charming extended phrase, in eighths and quarters with sustained half notes, and quietly expands this over the whole keyboard with an inwardly trembling stream of tones recalling cymbals and harps. When he begs the brook, the mill-wheels and the birds to cease their songs, because they can no longer compete with the jubilation of his voice, he nevertheless is fully aware of the poise of his own tune and does not extend the contour of his own melodic line beyond that of joyous contentment, with graceful short repetitions, with charming intervals used as accompaniment and with joyous beats signalling his delight in nature. Broad expansions on the theme proudly acknowledge his final possession; progressing harmonically, with an infinite flow of melodic invention, he pursues his way, returning with structural regularity to the point where he began; and rounds off the rhyme of the music more artistically than any rhyme of the text.

A pause. Graceful improvised sounds. This is the song to the lute which he hung on the wall, garlanded with a green ribbon. The accompaniment expresses contemplation, mystery, in the harmonies. This grows into a recitative of the brooding piano and is reflected in the voice, full of anxious presentiments. How unbound by formal requirements, this conception. This reminiscence of the pangs of love becomes in turn the prelude to new songs and is expanded beyond the confines of the verse into a pure expression of the overflowing heart, though this heart belongs only to the miller. The green band becomes a tiny Baroque episode. Green points the way to the hunter, but the color symbolisms of the text are of no real value to the musician. He has other means to color his art. He takes the sound of horns, transposed to the piano, to introduce the hunter. The jealous miller again takes up the sixteenths of the brook motive. He makes Schubert's task harder by telling the brook what should not be told to the miller's daughter. The "not" alters the significance of the melody, for it must be negative. Schubert ties a small knot, does away with the "not" and retains the grace of the melodic line by emphasizing all the more playfully the "*yes*" after the "*no*." "Tell her," he pipes in fine tunes and dances for the children, "Do tell her." And how does he treat the colors? Green breathes the fragrance of romance, as long as the milleress is amiable. When she is angry, then green implies the ominous. "Die böse Farbe" (The bad color) is a powerful moment of hatred projected upon Nature. The flour-dusted man despises himself. He has violent visions; helpless cries splinter the air; pale accents of despair, noisy horns, cursed farewells, fluttering green bands mingle in his tormented dreams. This piece expresses a tragic irony and is a masterpiece of changing moods. This little shifting of *no* and *yes* has created a cosmic picture of noble suffering. How poor the colors of the poet by comparison!

19. THE MILLER'S BEAUTIFUL DAUGHTER NO. 18, DEAD FLOWERS

The deep peace of maturity remains after the struggle. The time has come for one of the most gripping of all the melodies that Schubert wrote. Here we have the melancholy transposition from minor, over a delicate step, into major and back to minor; passing on to the second section with a wonderfully hesitating pointed rhythm reminiscent of her, and denoting a renewed hope of May. But at last there is the resigned descent into minor. The time has come for the poet to give the death blow to the miller. The latter addresses the brook, sweetly, simply. The brook answers him from its ordered rushing with heavenly grace. He picks up the sixteenths of the brook's motive and speaks to it again in the delicate emotional flow of the melody. And the brook intones a cradle song for him, an indescribable dream expressed in perfect music. A rocking tune, childlike, pious, wonderfully interwoven with the piano and repeated five times, like an ancient folk-song, until it sinks to rest in blessed peace. Now, however, the ocean encompasses the brook, the whole ocean, the whole of life. And Schubert touches his keys, his very own—quarters and eighths—harmonies tensed between the tonic and the dominant, raised to the ninth and suspended, never touching the earth; a noble and eternal song that reaches the very heights of "Tristan." The good miller in his brook has been sacrificed to one of the most essential inspirations of the composer.

Moritz von Schwind

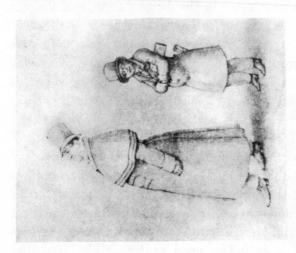

Michael Vogl and Franz Schubert go out to conquer. *Pencil sketch by Franz von Schober*

The market place in Steyr

The second cycle of poems written by Wilhelm Müller is the "Winterreise" (The Journey in Winter). Schubert wrote the music four years after "Die schöne Müllerin" and how he has developed, how much richer and deeper is the structural composition of this work! Yes, the mood is melancholy, full of mourning for his sweetheart. It is indeed the journey through ice and snow. Here again we have constant wandering against an ever changing background. And no music can travel forward as beautifully as Schubert's. For he possesses not only a talent for lyricism, but also the ability to carry the movement of the lyric mood through every emotion. These poems of Müller rank higher than the first group. They contain no forced metaphor, as earlier, between the miller, the brook and the colors; but they portray the natural expression of emotions, sometimes against a background of the surrounding world, but generally in an unforced and pure language which occasionally has the charm of folk-poetry.

Here we have no longer the mere singing; the air of the simple folk-song is not sufficient. The strophic repetition in the composition occurs less often. The mood conceived and composed as a whole is turned into a lyric entity which marks unusual transformation both in the grasp of the emotion and the inventiveness of expression.

We seem to see Schubert sitting before his note-paper and sketching his ideas with a light hand, flooded by the abundance of the forms that grow from text into music. A few graceful accompanying eighths, a painful, well-bound melody, and the "Gute Nacht" (Good Night) of the wanderer streams from the heart in the flow of rhythm and harmony. Here too the change from major to minor is a welcome means of obtaining slight alterations of mood within the given form, which is repeated. There is nothing sweeter than the switching of the major melody to the minor key, when he thinks of her dreaming, and the return to major when he bids her farewell—both so tender, so pianissimo, a Schubert pianissimo, a weird submerging into the pure depths of emotion. "Die Wetterfahne" (The Weather-Vane) turns, there is a unison in the painting of the piano and the progress of the voice with the accompaniment. How realistic this painting, with its few strokes; on the arpeggio of the piano the wind roams, turning to and fro in the phrases of the voice. Note here is a negative passage. Indoors the winds play with the emotions as they do outdoors on the roof, though not quite so loudly. "Not quite so loudly": the composer bridges the gap of the unmusical negation by inventing a *fermata* and a suspension of the voice within the contours of the melody which it carries. But this journey is already too melancholy to allow much room for spontaneous ironical gestures. The melancholy unity is scarcely disturbed, the music yields to it willingly without a smile.

The tuneful mourning of "Gefrorene Tränen" (Frozen Tears), this romantically stirring melody, experiences in its middle section the pain of dissonances for short moments. In a broad melody over moving triplets, starkness rises in tearful curves, with an indescribable balance between voice and instrument; the dream of the ice-flowers discloses the secret of a gentle, Chopin-like major-mood; and with a broad gesture the music returns to the painful tone of the beginning.

("Der Linderbaum.") The lindentree waves its leaves in a phrase of six sweet triplets followed by a graceful glance upward. The piano depicts this. The voice sings, as in an ancient song, of the well at the gate, where a lindentree stands; and the piano follows suit in simple imitation. The piano now ascends in a more expanded accompaniment, like echoing horn-blasts. Again the piano picks up the triplets of the lindentree and draws them into deeper shadow at the passage where "the cold winds blow." The phrase of the tree is picturesquely expanded, traces the steps of the emotion, roams chromatically through the trembling ache of memory. The poet says "My hat flew with the wind";

20. THE JOURNEY IN WINTER NO. 5, THE LINDEN TREE

the composer summons just the right rhythm for this line; and, in a circle, the piece returns to its beginning, for the tone-shading does not dominate the structure but merely enlivens it. This lindentree is an unforgettable part of all music. It is the ancestor of all the tree songs stemming from German Romanticism. As we read the text we are deeply moved by the visionary power of the music. Irrespective of periods or of fashions, the impetus of vision vibrates "Auf dem Flusse" eternally.

[98]

The stream is frozen; nor is the musician tempted by the lively phrase of its rush onward. The voice begins with simple chords and descends into a mystical minor, even softer than usual, ppp, the softest immersion occurring in any of Schubert's songs. The piano takes over the theme of the singer, actuated by his feeling. With concealed trembling the stream now mirrors the feelings of the human being just as it did so unaffectedly in summer. But winter causes the emotion to seek refuge within the soul. The landscape has no direct reflection in the flowing water. But, as if in memory, the landscape revives despite ice and numbness, with a mysterious compassion for man. Imagination cements this kinship with nature. Though the leaves of the lindentree be fallen, yet they rustle in memory of other days because the branches crackling in the cold winds produce this illusion. The stream still lives under the ice. Do you recognize your own picture? Is there just such turbulence under the heart's frozen surface?

Be it summer or winter, the musician leads his emotion into the whirlpool of sounds, and demands that nature answer him, directly and indirectly. How hastily the melody runs through the sixteenths as if to hasten its own end. "Irrlicht" (The will-of-the-wisp) tempts the composer to invent tone pictures in fluttering, vanishing phrases. With heavily moving chords the wanderer seeks repose and dreams of the spring.

21. THE JOURNEY IN WINTER NO. 11, THE DREAM OF SPRING

21. Winterreise

Nr. 11 Frühlingstraum

Etwas bewegt

Ich träum = te von bun = ten

Blu = men   so wie sie wohl blühen im Mai

"Frühlingstraum" (The Dream of Spring). How can we express all that is so spontaneously felt, all that is actually created here, all that the composer has reflected on this theme? Conquering the ice and the winds, he reaches the brook and the tree; and the spell is broken only when, at the peak of winter, the poet helps him to dream of flowers and green meadows. Like magic, this springlike melody ascends, the birds themselves emulating its gaiety. But alas, it is a dream! Already the piano frowns, the voice hesitates, torn by fright. The ice-flowers on the windows sound a warning, twice, in slow middle parts; indeed, they have the last word; though in the first instance the dream of spring revives, at the second repetition it is already extinguished.

The thrill of the quiet air in the midst of exciting storms; the picture of the speedy post-chaise, with -the beat of the heart echoing the trotting chords ("Die Post"); the fantastic vision of the greybeard ("Der Greise"), coming as an improvisation, partly recited; the flight of the crow (Die Krähe) depicted by the piano and the voice in fluttering sixteenths; the despairing music of "Letzte Hoffnung" (Last Hope) with its falling leaves and sorrow mounting bravely above the tomb; then suddenly the noise of the busy village ("Das Dorf"), a difficult musical picture inserted to create a contrast of moods; the tremendous short picture of the stormy morning ("Der stürmische Morgen"); the deception of the friendly light ("Irrlicht") which is so happily conceived with its juxtaposition of question and answer in the piano and the voice; the sign-post ("Der Wegweiser")—all these are new problems for Schubert's imagination and tempt him to create continually fresh forms of lyrical expression and musical interpretation. How wonderfully he makes use of the sign-post, which presents itself as immovable, to develop the phrase of the repeated note in a tone picture which begins like any commonplace piece of music and ends, like a prayer, in deep musical piety.

How tremendous a task is accomplished here! Language should not attempt to describe these compositions, each of which is a revelation of indestructible perfection. Whatever I say about them is superficial, hasty, a poor echo of what I feel about them, entirely inadequate to give the atmosphere of the pieces themselves. How I love the last four songs of the "Winterreise," and how can I impart this fondness to the reader, who will outreach my efforts just as soon as he can go to the piano and have the help of a friend, who will sing the songs for him? Then he is sure to exchange my words for the living reality of the music itself. Let him play the song called "Das Wirtshaus" (The Inn). He begins on the piano, very slowly, those truly Schubertian chords exhaling an everlasting German romanticism. The singer follows him with the melody beginning with the words: "My road has led me to the field of the dead. I thought: 'here I will rest for a while.'" Delight is infinite in noting how this melody within the circle of its being is developed, varied, raised to heights and led back to its beginning. Now the two performers will recover their gaiety in the piece called "Mut" (Courage), which is so virile and exploring in the combination and the arrangement of its parts, so fresh and joyous in its mood, especially in the major passage written to the words "gaily onward in the world, fighting wind and weather" (we find no other instance of such gaiety in the rest of the "Winterreise"). But here again we have the closing bars in the minor. And then "Die Neben-sonnen" (The Three Suns) appear. Weber antici-pated this in the warmth of the melody, sustained with so much feeling, in the beatitude of the re-peated suspended cadence descending in the inter-vals of thirds, a true characteristic of the romantic composer. This device has won continual praise for Schubert, but is ever novel and fresh since he in-vented it and loved to use it. At the end we have "Der Leiermann" (The Organ Grinder). Our players cannot limit their admiration. Though they have performed it often, they must admire once more the inconceivable delineation which con-tains, in spite of its simplicity, such a wealth of grace and feeling. Countless times they have said, and now they say it again, and I with them: this song seems not to have been created by the brain of man, but to have come into the world like the

22. THE JOURNEY IN WINTER NO. 24, THE ORGAN GRINDER

22. Winterreise

Nr. 24 Der Leiermann

Etwas langsam

Drü = ben hin = term Dor = fe steht ein Lei = er = mann

soil, the trees, and the grass. In the realm of art, it is as eternal as Nature itself. How did Schubert do this? He lets the left hand play the bass humming of the bagpipe, while the right hand plays a sad melody in folk-tone, a melody of touchingly short breath. The humming of the bagpiper goes on to the end while the voice, with scarcely any accompaniment, sings on, the song of the organ grinder, the artist, the empty plate. Occasionally the tone is varied with a short flourish, but on the whole the character remains the same. There is the monotonous humming of the bass, the drone of the pipe, the voice of the song. There is the voice of Schubert, the song of his life, his confession, quite simple and pure in empty space, very true, very sad—"Strange old man, shall I go with you, will you grind your organ while I sing my songs?" Only the voice brings these words to our ears. Never has the folk-tone been so nearly captured; never did Schubert do so much with such small means. These microcosms contained a universe.

Let us choose some of the songs written to poems by Goethe. Not by chance did Schubert find a staff in Goethe. When he wrote "Gretchen am Spinnrade" (Gretchen at the Spinning Wheel)—Opus 2 —he entered that musical atmosphere in which he was most prolific. But not only the young Goethe inspired him; he remained faithful to Goethe in his later work, and the "Westöstliche Divan," no less than "Faust" gave him material for successful compositions. Difficult though it was to establish personal contact between Goethe and Schubert, they are united in their work.

This "Gretchen am Spinnrade" became popular immediately, and has remained so. It stands at the beginning of Schubert's creations, in its complete-ness and maturity, and it reveals Schubert's tone especially in the charm and the breath of its senti-ment. "My peace is gone" was a welcome phrase

to which Schubert attached the repetitions and by
which he returned to the predetermined structure.
Of course he takes the movement of the spinning-

23. GRETCHEN AT THE SPINNING WHEEL, OPUS 2

wheel as the theme of the accompaniment. These sixteenths hum through the whole piece beneath the voice and are interrupted only at one point, where Gretchen speaks of his kiss; this is the natural climax of the composition. This song could serve as a model of the perfect wedding of inspiration and artistry. Gretchen's feeling for Faust is so beautifully balanced in the words and in the melody, develops so naturally in the harmonies, rises to such a telling crescendo, and at "the kiss" is so passionately sustained on a seventh chord, that the musical structure is as alive today as it ever was. And the whole song flows so naturally that we can scarcely understand why it ever seemed novel or epoch-making.

Do we understand this fact any better in "Der Erlkönig" (The Erkling)? It is known as Opus 1, as primary work of the type known as German "Lied," eternal, unsurpassed in the unwavering assurance of its musical quality. Again the piano is given the background. The triplets throb, describing the landscape. The air is stirred by rolling basses. Many characters appear—the poet, the father, the son, the Erlking. And the piano is modulated according to the speaker. With father, son and poet, the original triplets are retained, varied and harmonized according to the demands of the situation, now fuller, now lighter in tone,

24. THE ERLKING, OPUS 1 First Form

24. Erlfönig op. 1

Erfte Faffung

now hesitating, now crowding ahead. When the Erlking speaks the triplet becomes faster, either a tempting waltz movement or broken chords. At the close the busy wheels stop; the voice declares the tragic ending, recitative. All this would be of lesser importance if the flow of the whole were not so smooth that lights and shadows seem to play on one level, as it were. Every dissonance, every incongruity, whether of humor or harmonic shading, put in even at the risk of being out of keeping (as for instance when the Erlking breaks into

Schubert, Lachner, Schwind and Vogl, serenading a newly built
house. *Pen and ink sketch by Moritz von Schwind, 1862*

An evening in Grinzing; Schubert, Lachner and Bauernfeld enjoying a bottle of wine. *Pen and ink sketch by von Schwind, 1862*

the triplets of the riding father and son) is welded into an organic whole such as music alone can give us.

May I point in a few words to the many sidedness of some of the other Goethe songs? I deplore further analysis and mere recounting, but I am afraid of omitting something that may be significant to the mental portrait of Schubert. I am not playing the rôle of music teacher in this book. I have been asked to draw a musical likeness of Schubert, not to forget any of the features that are important in his artistic delineation or significant in perpetuating him in our grateful memory. Has one any inkling of the multiplicity of shapes that arise from his songs? He has touched all the registers of singing humanity. Take, from the Goethe songs, "Meeresstille" (Ocean Peace), this broad flow of the voice, just the voice over long-drawn-out arpeggios, gleaming quietly in their structural strength. Take "Heidenröslein" (Heather Rose), this marvel of a folk-song, not imitated but felt as folk music, that, had it sprung from earth itself, could not be more sincere or simpler in tone. Take "Erster Verlust" (First Loss), how full of sentiment the lovely melody sings to the lively accompaniment, how the well known chords and phrases speak a new language of the soul, and how touchingly the voice in the **major** passes into the minor finale of the accompaniment.

Schubert's personality has endless variety. In "Der König von Thule" (The King of Thule) we find a delicate mixture of legend and folk-song, just a little bit exotic and, withal, so natural that we could not conceive it otherwise. "Wer nie sein Brot mit Tränen ass" (Who never ate his bread with tears); these words lead him on untraveled paths, the piano improvises dreamily; the song evolves sorrowful sevenths, solemn chords and, at the words "he enters life and becomes guilty" he puts *guilty* in the minor and, seizing the opportunity given by the words "all guilt must be expiated on earth," he lets the voice repeat the words in a high curve and permits the piano alone to sink into an abyss of unrelieved melancholy.

"Suleika," written much later, opens new paths. Formal text does not prevent him from following the easy flow of his inventive genius. Before the voice even begins, the rhythm of the musical structure is definitely fixed. The glad tiding, brought from the East, is turned into a graceful movement, dreamy and reflective, to which the words seem to fit of their own accord. At the end, they are set to a somewhat slower pace. The ingenuity with which he clothes an abstract text in rhythmic emotion is no less than the inspiration of all the budding folk-songs. The same may be said of the other

poem from the "Westöstlicher Divan," which is
called "Geheimes" (Secret Things). It is admirable to see how Schubert sets these words, so full of
meaning, on the graceful rhythm of a two-fourths
measure, which is like short beating of wings, like
a scherzo, like a secret round of the fairies, all light
and breath, air and gesture, and yet embellished as
are the Suleika songs, with detailed drawings full
of grace, variety and ascending force.

"An Schwager Kronos" (To Father Time) is a
prelude to Wagner. We must not forget the heroic,
the mighty Schubert, in spite of his winning grace.
Had he remained alive, these are the qualities that
he would have developed. With his death, time was
left to develop them. The romantic composers
heard this strain and shaped their work to its
measure. For the piano alone, it suggests a mighty
picture of a rattling, rolling journey into the
depths of earth. It contains force, push, and impetus, and its heavy accents rumble upon unruly
measures. It rises to the pathos of heavy chords,
which solemnly eclipse each other and are sustained
by sword and victory motives. The world of the
Nibelungen seethes in it. In Schubert's own style,
there occurs the passage of the girl, the happy moment, the foaming drink, placed, as contrast, just
before a still more elemental repetition of thun-
dering tones, of beating points, of the heroic trum-

pet blasts, which the voice, piercing the waving wall of music, interprets freely almost in recitative.

Let us mention the song "Ganymed" as an example of Schubert's skill in illustrating musically a succession of moods, a series of movements. Its intellectual power is of the highest. There is already a forecast of Hugo Wolf in it. Now the voice pursues its purely musical inclinations, now the accompaniment travels its own ways; finally the two join. On this path, winding so deftly between formality and imagination, between intellectuality and tone-painting, are found, as by chance, blossoms so new in shape and color, in melody and harmony, that the future can still find new joy in them.

"Uber allen Gipfeln ist Ruh" (Peace on the Heights). Inventive genius is spurred on by these few lines. The piano plays a simple Schubertian movement. The voice takes it up like a song. Language and mood are born. The voice speaks and forms the melody from the intonation, from the punctuation of the text. The piano creeps along syncopically. Rhythms unite again. "Wait, soon you too will rest," results in an inevitable tone-setting. Soft sound of softest words. The voice goes to rest, the piano follows. It is a brief intense musical picture, the more masterly in form because of its narrow confines.

The six songs that Schubert composed based on texts by Heine are among his happiest. It is readily understood that this poet, with his tendency to imitate the folk-tone, tempted Schubert particularly. But it does not follow that he was influenced by Heine in acquiring a freer dramatic style, a step toward the German romantic opera. It is true that Schubert passed through an evolution in this respect, but not in the form as much as in the intensity of this expression. The dramatic form of song may be noted in his earliest productions, just as the definitely lyrical form may be found among his latest. In fact, the very last song that he wrote, "Die Taubenpost" (The Pigeon Post) is not a bit more developed in formal style than similar humorous pieces of his early years.

"Der Atlas" (Atlas) belongs to the mournful, heavily burdened songs. Here unhappiness and pride let the piano have a dark rhythmical foundation over which the voice is carried in a far-flowing line whose direction is influenced only by the changes of expressions and development. "Ihr Bild" (Her Picture) is more restrained in the economical use of a few effective chords and modulations, and often brings the voice into a unison with the piano; the hopelessness of the episode is given but scanty emotional warmth in the middle of the piece by means of the dream, secretly re-

membered. "Das Fischermädchen" (The Fisher-
maiden) inclines to the style of the old "Lied." It
becomes a charming barcarolle, floating on equally
charming harmonies and swinging chords, and lets
the melody flatter our ear with its tender southern
melancholy.

25. THE FISHER MAIDEN
25. Das Fischermädchen

The song called "Die Stadt" (The Town) is
one of Schubert's cleverest tone-pictures. The
words paint the town with its towers, appearing
on the far horizon wrapped in fog, as it were, by
the falling evening shadows. He dares his delineation by means of diminished sevenths which rise

and fall in ghostly waves above a trembling bass. The song itself moves to heavy pointed chords. Later it interrupts its narrative with a phrase of sevenths, closing with the original form; whereupon the piano alone goes on with the sevenths. Here we have a unique combination of tone-painting and song, of formal style and impressionistic composition. Not unlike this is the composition of the song "Am Meer" (By the Sea). The piano in this case begins with heavily dragging harmonies that indicate the background. At the words "the sea gleamed far out" voice and piano together begin the sweet contemplative melody. Suddenly there is a transition to dramatic action; the fog rises to the tremoli of the piano, while waters roar, the sea-gull flies, and tears flow in mournful suspensions back to the pure melodic line; then the round is repeated from the very start and ends with a closing phrase in the traditionally formal cadence, not unlike that by which Brahms with proper meekness ends his songs. The piano, however, adds the same mystical chords with which it began, as a final touch to this short unified drama.

In a less complicated manner, the "Doppelgänger" (The Double) gives a similarly moving dramatic picture without emphasizing the contrasts. The "Stille Nacht" (Peaceful Night) is the bearer of softly gliding harmonies, above which the

26. BY THE SEA

26. Am Meer

voice grows livelier. Memory becomes the echo by which the piano imitates the voice. When shudders arise at the sight of the poet's mirrored reflection, the harmonies are changed to frightening dissonances and abrupt modulations. The close is quite lyrical with a phrase whose essence is reconciliation. These Heine songs! They are the goal of all those paths which Schubert's imagination pursued. In them complete devotion to melody joins hands with fidelity of delineation. Nor is one of these qualities given greater prominence than the other.

Their classic style is based on the rooted balance of character and beauty.

I would like to release the reader from following me further into the realm of the "Lieder." Has he grown weary? I confess that I can never be. To get a glimpse of the true, the real Schubert, one must approach him by the path of the songs. In the last analysis they are a complete self-confession. This form was granted him to express intimacy with grandeur and to make the grand gesture with grace. In them he solved problems of musical composition which in other cases are left lying on a fallow field. We wander, as through a forest, where many well-known beautiful spots invite us to rest. Or we are surprised to find new places, of whose existence we did not dream. "Frühlingssehnsucht" (Longing for Spring) is one of the Rellstab poems, which has been incorporated in the last group, the so-called "Swan-songs." "Rustling winds, so lightly blowing," breathe through so many of his songs, but nowhere more tenderly and more airily depicted than in this little masterpiece. The music sweeps along with the text. Where there are questions, rests and memories, the harmonies kindly stop for a moment, subsequently to join the onward flow which plays around us even more pleasantly than before. Movement and rest, matter and mind, how infinitely varied are the ways in which they are combined! And what about Rellstab's "Serenade"? Who still remembers that Rellstab wrote the text? This tune has become so famous that one scarcely remembers that Schubert composed it. Here he had an extraordinary inspiration. An accompaniment as if played by guitars, somewhat Spanish in tone, ecstatic, lovesick, and yet so pure in style; though we may examine the structure of this song, touch its joints, its protuberances, its secret places, we cannot understand the miracle of its effectiveness.

27. THE SERENADE

27. Ständchen

Tavern "Gottweigerhof," where Schubert lived in 1823

Johann Jenger, Anselm Huettenbrenner and Schubert. *Colored
drawing by Teltscher, about 1827*

The "Wanderer" appears to us a slow "Erl-king" with triplets, curved contours of the basses, voice in recitative. But the development is quite different. The essence of the song becomes clear in the middle section, in those few lines of melody which Schubert took as his motto wherever he expressed romantic longing. There are lively passages, emotions are roused at a faster pace; but suddenly there is return to the slow movement, the voice comes back to creeping triplets. Here we have dramatic movement within lyrical peace. But the combinations of these two are infinite. "Der Tod und das Mädchen" (Death and the Maiden) for instance gives us movement within rest, of a deeper significance. Death receives from Schubert's hand those slowly moving chords, a half note with two quarters so beloved by him; chords of death which pursued him into the realm of chamber music. Interrupting, the maiden begs Death not to touch her for she is still young. Here are two lines of brief dramatic excitement which Death quells at last. Death who moves with the self-same chords through the voice, through the piano with the voice, and alone in the piano.

"Dem Unendlichen" (To the Eternal)—Klopstock's solemnity is related to the noble romanticism of Wolfram. "Des Sangers Habe" (The Poet's Wealth)—to the strains of the Nibelungs. "Im

Frühling" (In the Spring)—what airy grace of
dancing rhythms. "Abendbilder" (Pictures of the
Evening)—the old phrase of the "Lindentree" is
expanded into a long-drawn-out mood full of hidden secrets. "Der Zwerg" (The Dwarf)—this song
was unknown to me until I heard it sung by Lulu
Muys Gmeiner and was transported by the dramatic vision which employed the most commonplace objects to evoke the deepest musical impressions. "Die Forelle" (The Trout)—here we are
at the frontier of chamber music where the floating gurgling theme taken from the song is elevated
to absolute music. Yes, soon we have reached
chamber music; our eye no longer perceives the
materiality of the enunciated text, words disappear,
content vanishes and the unaltered pure power of
music holds its sway. "Der Einsame" (The Lonely
One)—here we recognize, among many humorously dancing pieces, a "moment musical" this time,
by chance, with text. "Hymne an die Jungfrau"
(Hymn to the Virgin)—the blessed melody of the
Ave Maria. Was it written for the voice or for the
strings? "Du bist die Ruh" (Thou art Peace)—the
absolute beauty of the melody, which has become
historical, will always surpass the artificiality of
Rückert's text. "Auf dem Wasser zu singen" (To
be sung on the water)—Where do the gleam and
flow of the water in their rushing confusion of

28. Die Allmacht THE ALMIGHTY

dancing sixteenths glisten more brightly: in the piano or in the impatient voice? "Die Allmacht" (The Almighty) redeems us through the noble style of the oratorium interrupted by softly lyrical passages. The words, be they Latin or German, are there only as bearers of an exalted sentiment which, with outstretched palms, invokes all the elements of music to celebrate the pure divinity of the Lord. The words become vassals of the musician and make their obeisance to him.

CHAMBER MUSIC

INTIMATE natures incline to Chamber Music. It is not desecrated by words as singing is, nor has it the pretensions of an orchestra. It conducts itself, as it were. The players are only differentiations of a single soul which expresses itself in different instruments. They must feel in unison in order to be able to play. But they do not feel, as do singer and accompanist, in different varieties of musical speech, but in one and the same language—a language which is merely decomposed into a number of instruments. The nearer these instruments are to one another, as in the string quartet, the more perfect is the ensemble in its diversified unity and its unified variety. If the piano is added to the strings, two worlds face one another; on the one hand the world of harmony, of the broken tone; on the other, the melodic world of the sustained tone. Whatever is lost in unity is replaced by the possibilities of contrast. However, the ultimate refinement, the final refuge of the composer who wants to escape from a trivial presentation will always be in the noble abstraction of the string quartet.

Schubert grew up among such beliefs. From earliest youth he had the opportunity to hear chamber music and to practice it. To the intimate charm of this form of musical expression was added the ease of having it performed. He could actually hear whatever he wrote and thus control it. He was not dependent on the inclination or the disinclination of a singer, but could base his work on the well-founded, businesslike and continuous organization of a chamber music society, which was personal enough to be interested in him and yet sufficiently impersonal to follow the routine of duty.

Schubert's chamber music exhausts every possibility of this form of instrumentation. Whenever the piano is added, he knows how to produce a contrast to the strings with the surety of genius: he understands how to develop each accentuation, each passage of the instruments, so that the strings are not only supplemented but woven into the larger aspect of the tone picture. The strings, on the other hand, always retain their characteristic range and tone, and are full of that skill and technique which the custom and practice of the period allowed. The essential feature always remains the same—the manifoldness, the variety of the ensemble which translates the musical idea into the diversified language of the instruments and shapes

the movement of the musical piece out of the very
nature of the instruments. This is particularly interesting in the strophic repetition of the themes,
which occurs two or three times according to the
number of the performing instruments. But it is
not only that. The magic of tone is there, too. The
intuitiveness of Schubert's musical ear establishes
rhythmical and harmonic combinations, between
the piano and the strings and among the strings
themselves, which offer to our delighted senses
hitherto unknown secrets of tone combinations and
range of tones. Mere virtuosity is always absent.
The primary position of the first violin, which
characterized the early string quartet, has been
overcome. Ever feudal regulation is put aside in
favor of a democratic equality of all the performers. On the contrary, there is special grace in giving the four players the lead in the melodies, in
varying the latter according to the character of
each instrument and according to the progress of
the piece and the final unison with one another. In
addition, the content of these pieces has clearly
departed from the formal theory of classic writing. Schubert is wary of all theories. He does not
like themes which are confined to mere presentation of an idea. The themes have, as it were, a
second meaning, a mental allusion, a rustic background, a reminiscence of folksong or folk-dance.

In short, they are romantic; they speak, they express themselves in gestures, they possess the will to formulate innermost experiences and similes.

29. SONATA: PIANO WITH VIOLIN, OPUS 137, I
LAST MOVEMENT

29. Sonate Klavier mit Violine op. 137,1
Letzter Satz

The well known short sonatas for piano and violin, opus 137, 1–3, show in miniature the method of working. Let us look at the distribution of themes. Every possibility of introducing primary themes is employed. The first sonata begins by having the piano and the violin play the first theme in unison. In the second sonata the piano alone begins a long-spun theme which is then taken up by the violin with the accompaniment of the piano in a changed and shortened form. In the third sonata, both instruments again start in with a thematic prelude which is first developed by the piano in the form of a song and then carried right over into the second theme with the bass of the piano joined to the violin. Thus the first sonata is more schematic in its construction; the second and the third are freer; but the third is a compromise between the first and second methods.

But such formal matters cannot detain for long if we love Schubert's special characteristics. The construction of these sonatas may adhere more or less closely to rules as they have been laid down. It is the loveliness of the ideas, the elegance of the execution, the surprise of a sudden harmony which charms us again and again. Even though the form of these pieces be pretty rather than majestic, there is all of Schubert in the ease with which the themes run into each other, the grace with which they are joined, in the modest pride and the timid emotion of the *crescendi* and the *ritardandi*. Untiring melodies run over Schubert's strings—an *espressivo* on the violin accompanied by the *pianissimo* chords of the piano, as in the middle of the slow movement of the D Major Sonata: then the Rondo flying along, teasingly, with an incomprehensible variety, as a final movement; or the chain of themes in the A Minor Sonata, the beautiful song of the Andante with the repeated breaths of the violin, the agile final movement of the A Minor, which remains a rondo in its always graceful return of the theme;

the mighty uplift of the Andante in the G Minor
Sonata, which sums up all the figure-work in an
elemental picture of far-reaching harmonies, the
gay folk-melody in the last movement—Though
the frame be narrow, piano and violin can scarcely
have a wider range of expression than imagination
grants them in these instances. But this is only the
beginning.

PIANO TRIO, OPUS 99, FIRST MOVEMENT

The piano trio in B Flat Major begins by letting the three instruments join in a precise enunciation of the theme. Violin and 'cello take up in unison this virile hornlike theme which smacks of the soil, and the piano gives it the rhythm with accentuated eighths which are enlivened by pointed basses. The violin sweeps along the theme in a run of sixteenths towards the bass, and the 'cello answers in a run of sixteenths towards the treble. Thus the idea is clearly announced. It is immediately repeated an octave higher in C Minor until the strings show an inclination to separate their voices in a slight degree. At this point the resolution of the theme is begun. For the moment the piano does not participate in it. It only lends the rhythm. But violin and 'cello alternately take up the theme until nothing remains of it but a gesture which is quickly taken up by the piano and carried to the bass in runs. The strings, on the other hand, reverse the order and carry the movement forward chromatically from bass to treble till the piano takes up the movement and the original B Flat Major is reached at last. At this point the reverse order begins; the piano has the main theme and the strings have the accompaniment. How normal is the course of this beginning! With a clarity which adds to the musical richness, the distribution and variation of thematic content is shown in the character of the different instruments and in the rise and fall of the cadence. We may regard a piece like this as a short drama. It no longer is the easy play of the sonatina; the instruments confront one another with solemn symphonic consciousness, each presenting its thoughts, interchanging them and performing at the same time that strange rhythmical dance in which the lines of the melodies are interwoven and disentangled on the terraces of the harmonies.

Let us see how Schubert introduces his second theme in this trio. The piano has reached A in its chromatic run which it performs solo. It picks up this A and leaves it to the 'cello which in its turn sings the A quite alone, a high A, expanding it mightily, then letting it drip down three times, finally using it to begin, pianissimo, an F Major melody which is accompanied by the piano with broken chords. Here is a truly Schubertian melody, first swinging the sixth up and down, then doing the same with the seventh, then cadencing into a delightful figure. But already the violin rises higher, and repeats the theme in unison with the 'cello, and carries it along above the chords with a mighty sweep, and glides down again to be taken up by the piano for a third time and led to repose in a still wider curve. The rhythm is set; the strings rejoice in it; the piano gives it sharper accent, and soon the point is reached where we turn back to

Schubert evening at the home of Josef von Spaun. *Sketch in oil by Moritz von Schwind, 1868*

FR. SCHUBERT

Schubert, from a lithograph by Josef Teltscher, 1826

the beginning. But we are in minor now. The mighty development, first with the first theme, then with the second added, becomes a more and more crowded interplay of these rhythms and melisms until the piano calls for a last display of energy in a proudly pointed phrase. Again the search begins pianissimo through the instruments and the various keys, and at last the beginning is really attained, the circle is closed; the piano holds the theme which the strings announced before as a prelude, and holds it closely, and the first movement accomplishes its predestined fate.

The Andante of this trio is based entirely on a barcarolle-like rhythm, partly cradle song, partly Venetian boat song, which the piano pronounces at the very beginning so that we may not forget it. The 'cello begins with the melody two measures further on. This melody is of incomparably dreamlike softness. At several points it sinks to sweetly diminished chords as on a resilient cushion. The violin picks up this tune while the 'cello continues playing. There arises that ever pleasing polyphonic harmony of singing voices which spur one another on towards beauty. Later the piano also tries to express this melody with the means at its command. But what can it do in a contest with strings? It is merely a dry outline which the strings must animate with their song. And soon the piano withdraws to being the accompaniment of the swinging rhythm over which the strings weave their melody closer and closer. Suddenly, in the middle movement, the piano finds the right path. It no longer competes with the strings. Garlands of rapid coloratura are scattered profusely with one or both hands over a new syncopated theme which the piano carries in part. But the strings will not let go their hold. They participate in this coloratura work and, out of rhythm and flourish, there is created an infinitely ornamented picture of rising and falling tracing of voices.

I want to place special emphasis on certain parts of this drama, on scenes in which a particularly interesting interweaving of motives occurs. The Scherzo of this trio has a Beethoven-like agility in the way the voices follow one another. And the Trio of the Scherzo is so full of Schubert's skill in composing waltzes that we see his best side. The last Rondo, however, is a pyrotechnic display of popular melodies and is a charmingly humorous close to the dramatic development of the piece. Violin and piano begin with a mocking game in which the 'cello joins suddenly, laughing its part, as it were. The piano joins hands, all three dance the round. The end is a general somersault. The violin hums a tune, the piano continues dancing. Suddenly we hear a strange melody accompanied by the descending tremolo of the piano, a melody like the shaking up and down of arms, the babbling of drunken voices, half Slavic, half Hungarian, so strange in its tone that no accompaniment seems to be right for it except this trembling echo of the piano. But everything quickly grows normal; the dance continues. The strange melody returns, only this time its distribution is reversed. The unison stops. Bits of the first themes fly through the air; the violin announces something: here it comes, in 3/2 time, an extraordinarily turned rhythm, with tremendous breath, and long steps. Imagination is given full play in the three instruments. Then it retraces its steps. The old themes are thrown helter-skelter, as well as the measures, 2/4 and 3/2, and, as if it would never end, it turns again and again on its own axis, leaps into the air, and sings on until an abrupt presto sweeps away the whole affair.

The second piano trio, in E Flat Major, is as significant as the first. Both these pieces belong to the greatest of Schubert's works. They date from his most intensive period, 1827, and in them he reveals as much of the unconditional mastery of technique as of the ultimate reality of his form of expression. I do not know whether the first or the second trio is the more romantic. They are both romantic in their idyllic dramatization. I do not know whether, as Schubert says, the first trio is more feminine and the second more masculine. Both of them are a rare mixture of proud and tender emotions. Perhaps the second is more real in expressing that Schubert-like characteristic which indicates the liberation from formulas of the classic period in order to turn towards folk music, that quality of Schubert which seeks breath and life in rhythms and songs of the soil. The first theme of Opus 99 was assuredly more pastoral in character than the formal first theme of Opus 100. But the second theme of the latter was much more formal in the treatment of the instruments than the second theme of the former, which beats the ground heavily, given over to the unbounded joy of the dance. The progression of themes in the second trio is unbelievably profuse. They do not conform so much to formal construction as to the errant waves of the imagination, which is continually conjuring up new combinations from the old world of sounds. Perhaps there is an elusive interrelation between parts of the themes, but this is not accentuated; the themes have their own being, stretched out in the field among the instruments and full of the scent of unaccustomed harmonies. In exuberant measures they praise their own existence, for pages and pages, in ever novel variations and repetitions.

The Andante of the E Flat Major Trio grew into a separate movement. It is based on a folk-melody, which is said to be Swedish. The melody is delicate and tender in mood and shows a beautiful line in the development of its various parts till it reaches its arched and slightly cadenced close. Its foundation is a hesitating, creeping rhythm, with

PIANO TRIO, OPUS 100

31. Klaviertrio op. 100

strangely pointed *forzati*. The 'cello announces it
for the first time. As it is long, the violin does not
repeat the melody at once, but the piano takes it
up and the two strings have the accompaniment
which was at first indicated by the piano. Soon the
tone picture expands. Like a chain, the burden of
the melody is woven between the strings. The piano
harmonizes like an accompaniment. The rhythm
resounds and, over arpeggios, we return to the beginning. A small piece of the theme reappears, but
the hand of the ballad-maker turns to new harmonies. Just as in one of Schubert's songs, where a
simple tune depicts a tragic fate, the symphony
of the three instruments is spread out till it becomes a mighty landscape growing to giant propor-
tions. Then comes a recapitulation, the theme of
the song, a vignette, and the end.

I leave the fairly canon-like Scherzo, with the
mad rhythms of its middle movement and the
pleasant rondo motion of the last part with its
gayly repeated theme and its other amenities, to
the kind treatment of the chamber music player.
Whether he be at the many-fingered piano, at the
light-toned violin or at the deep-voiced 'cello, he
will never grow tired of playing this scene under
Schubert's direction with all the detail that has
been given it. But this andante is a source of real
anxiety for me. There are times when words fall

flat confronted by the magic of sound. This happens continually when one attempts to describe the greatest music. I read such music even as I write. I can go on describing it to the point where the music reaches that part of my being where it remains at rest in the meaning of its absolute, tonal life. Then I am nearest to the spirit of Schubert. And then I lay down my pen and wait.

Schubert's piano quintet for piano, violin, viola, 'cello and contrabass (this latter instrument seldom used in such combination) has become famous under the name of "Forellenquintett" (Trout Quintet) because he used the theme of the song "Die Forelle" (The Trout) for one movement. Something of the rustic mood of the song has passed over into the other movements as well. It was written in the country and it exhales the very odor of Nature. It is an unassuming piece which is played very often because it is a grateful task and easily impressive. It is not as important as the trios for piano. Schubert lets the stream of music flow on, freely yielding to chance thoughts and the play of imagination, and he possesses the masterly technique enabling him to shift the tones to the five instruments without much subtlety or pedantry.

The themes of the first movement are simple, song-like, lyrical, and are wound up in a web of flourishes and runs, the soft breezes of Nature itself. The voices are singing; light runs are interwoven; trills rejoice; suspensions indicate brief longings. In the development the composition is somewhat confused, but neatly arranged dance-rhythms make for easy progress. Melody blossoms beautifully in the slow movement, and the syncopated ascents that interrupt it lend a Viennese mood to the dance. The whole atmosphere of the piece is Viennese, a waltz mood breathes throughout the Scherzo.

32. TROUT QUINTET, OPUS 114

32. Forellenquintett op. 114

Now the "trout theme" appears. It is an inserted movement, so that we find five instead of four movements in this piece, a very rare occurrence at that time. If Schubert happens to write only two movements, one readily speaks of the composition as of something "unfinished." When he writes five,

there is no surprise about it. The trout song movement is made up of a set of variations. It is always
somewhat difficult for us today to be moved by
this artificial alteration of a theme which assumes
different masks, one after the other. But it is genuine, being based on the structural character of old
music. Nothing happens in this case except that
Schubert grows fond of a theme and expands it
according to established rules. One must not assume a psychological attitude in judging this form.
Psychology, that interesting disease, did not affect
music until a later period. The "trout theme" is
first announced by the four strings, while the piano
is silent. Then the piano advances with a slightly
ornamented variation of the theme, and the strings
have the accompaniment. By slow degrees we come
to understand the inner purpose and meaning of
the variation. It gives full play to technical skill
for the very reason that it is allowed to be un-
psychological. Now the violin shines out above the
viola, which sustains the theme, seconded by the
piano. Then the piano shines out above the basses
of the strings, which have taken up the theme. A
fever of variations soon takes hold of all five instruments as they transpose the theme to the minor
and let it run away in a mighty sea of sounds. The
strings, accompanied playfully by the plashing of
the piano, play a variation in freer form of the

minor echoes of the main theme. Again there comes
a return to the major key, the violin picks up the
original theme, the piano running along with the
same leaping flourish as in the song. The 'cello repeats the theme, the violin does the same with
the flourish of the piano, the second part brings the
same alternations, and the end fades away in the
watery figure of the accompaniment.

In the Finale all this gaiety is crowned with an
arrangement of merry dances which are a compromise between the Bohemian and the Viennese
mood. These dances are distributed among all the
instruments with charming pertness and begin over
and over again. Hand in hand, the blithe round
comes to an end.

A great number of Schubert's chamber music
pieces are lying about—the rondo for piano and
violin, so strange in its modulations and rhythms,
that early trio for the piano which was discovered
by chance only a short time ago, the string quartets
of Schubert's youth, so rich in content, through
which the master first attained his growth. Now
and then we pick up a piece and are touched by
the graceful charm of each line and each musical
phrase, but we always return to the essential, important works in which his art created its eternal
image. The piano now assumes a minor part. It
has played a dominant rôle in the chamber music

compositions because, thanks to its broad harmony, it supplied the strings with the firm basis of balanced music. Now the pure string quartet is organized, that most absolute form of abstract music, in which everything depends on the ensemble of voices; abstract thought expressed in a chorus of strings. Schubert's work in the quartet reaches its highest point in three creations, which belong to the deathless expressions of musical emotion, because in them (and in a different manner in each) there has been erected a unified architecture absolute in its perfection.

The A Minor Quartet is the easiest. It sports its gay themes simply and gracefully. It is incomprehensibly delicate in its construction. What a beginning! Viola and 'cello have a distinctly pushing beat in the bass. Above them, the second violin has a creeping broken harmonic rhythm in accompanying eighths. After listening to this for the time of two measures, the first violin, breathing gently, carries the melody. A figure in thirds and accented trills forms the transition to the second theme that proves a pleasant complement in the major key. The development, whether it be rhythmic or melodic, does not omit any one of these motives and interweaves them happily. What an unagitated picture is presented by such a score! It may be compared to a tree with the strong

33. STRING QUARTET IN A MINOR, OPUS 29,
FIRST MOVEMENT

33. Streichquartett A-Moll op. 29. Erster Satz

trunk, as the bass parts, the branches as the middle parts, the blossoms as the trebles, and yet it is so arranged that no high or low is more apparent. Unity is attained in the reflection of the various themes, a unity which far surpasses that of Nature.

Schubert has used no other motive quite as often as this. It was first used in "Rosamunde," then in the Andante of this quartet, then in the Im-

Inn "Zum Goldenen Rebhuhn"

The Karlskirche (Church) with the Technical High School (to the right) and Fruhwirth mansion (to the left). The buildings front on the River Wien

Schubert, from the oil painting by Joseph Mähler, about 1827

34. STRING QUARTET IN A MINOR, OPUS 29, SECOND MOVEMENT

34. Streichquartett A=Moll op. 29. Zweiter Satz

Andante

promptus for Piano. One has to admit it is as Schubertian as possible in its broadly dancing rhythm as well as its sweetly scented melody. What he does with it here, in the quartet, beggars description. After the theme has been established, the motion goes on interweaving and enlacing, with untiring smoothess and pliability of melodic line and harmonic coloring. The original theme peeps out again; it questions the four parts and then begins its second course to heightened movement in sixteenths. It spreads out its arms like a symphony. Once more it has a reminiscence of its original form and then bids us farewell with a moving chorus in which all the voices participate.

It is a common experience (corroborated by the

books) that, when describing Schubert's music, one is able to transpose into language the first two movements with much greater exactness than the last. This is not Schubert's fault. It must be attributed to the inability of language to penetrate further into the construction of these movements. These may be described as the simple composition of a scherzo in which the essence of its being is fulfilled by the contrast of the trio, or as a finale in which charming songs and dances are combined in a graceful and almost disorderly mixture. The Menuet of the A Minor Quartet is one of the most entrancing pieces of Viennensia that Schubert ever composed. To revel in it one must hear that bird-like tirra-lirra on one note, that yodling, those roguish beats on one note after another, the timid peasant dance in the Trio. Nor is the last movement different, though it be somewhat Hungarian in coloring. It is transparent until we come to the *unisono*. Then it is steeped in the full sonority of the voices, which is accomplished by a subtle management of the middle parts. This first theme skipping along, this pointed second theme, and ever again the roguish return, playful, looking about, leading astray, the symphonic escape and the return to the beloved dance measure—Schubert might repeat it ten times more if he chose and we would never tire of it.

35. STRING QUARTET IN D MINOR, FIRST MOVEMENT

35. Streichquartett D=Moll. Erster Satz

The second famous quartet is written in D Minor. It is much more serious and conceived on a more grandiose scale. For its main theme it has the rhythm of a beat following upon a triplet, and therefore many people are reminded by it of Beethoven's C Minor Symphony and regard it as a song of fate, corroborated in this opinion by the fact that it contains the variations on "Death and

[145]

the Maiden." But one must not go too far. It would be an easy task to depict in words the fateful adventures to which the hero of this quartet has to submit. Words come to us easily enough when we hear it—if we happen to be present at a performance of the quartet the day before we have to write about it. We seem already to have mastered the language in which we wish to portray the music. But the fact is, that when we have to set the words down, they lose their force. The more musical the music, the less potent the words—especially in the case of Schubert, whose goal is the essence of music, not its meaning. How manifold are the forms of the triplet theme in that first movement! It lives vividly in the crossing of the parts; it roams through the score, now high, now low, now joined, now contrasted; it forms the rhythmical foundation of the second theme, which seems to begin in a song peacefully swinging along, but soon colors the triplets of this movement, which is shot through and through with rhythm, with sorrowful contours and crowded polyphony. This movement is one of Schubert's greatest poems. It is a unified organism, unequalled in movement, composition, beginning and resolution of its close; the unity of its invention arising out of an incredibly profound intuition.

The variations of the second movement on the theme of "Death and the Maiden" scarcely present a problem of psychological content. There is enough spirituality in the development of this music which, in the course of all its changes, by the varied play of its energies, by the enchantment of its details, is carried back to the original homely theme in slow diminution. Such a happening is purely musical. The choice of the theme is due to love of it *per se,* not to any hidden desire to be operatic. Did Wagner think of the Scherzo when he created Mime? The quartet has Mime's theme, even two themes which belong to Mime's world. But the connection here is in invention, not in meaning. What is made of the theme, in this case or in that, is something entirely different. In the history of music, no less than in the work of the individual composers, we find similar themes. Schubert himself often composes in closely related phrases, whose correlation need not be purposely planned.

Let us glance at the presto of the D Minor Quartet. Here is a movement similar to the first movement, because its rhythm, that rustic skipping motive, runs through the whole as with held breath. Now it rushes along *unisono,* then dances away suddenly in chords, and becomes the accompaniment of a three-eighths theme which in its turn roams about and then carries new melodies. Eternal play, eternal dance.

36. STRING QUARTET IN G MAJOR,
FIRST MOVEMENT

36. Streichquartett G=Dur. Erster Satz

Schubert has given us fifteen string quartets. The last, in G Major, surpasses them all in splendor of orchestration. In this piece we have an intimation of Schubert's future. Here we can see how high he would have flown if longer life had been granted him. The four instruments are almost over-burdened. The force of dramatic representation which bursts from them almost causes them to shudder. Who dares to be tired or discouraged when he sees the veils lifted from secrets of which romanticism had no inkling? Composed in ten days, this music lays bare paths which no one could have

[148]

imagined. In none of Schubert's symphonies is there room for so much. What freedom there is in the initial gesture! What impetus there is in the pointed themes, set so precisely in major and minor, a contrast which formerly signified merely a gentle confession. Weird tremblings sweep the strings. A theme taken from a Viennese dance is expanded with elemental demonic strength. Syncopes beat the measure in the second theme which the 'cello later on introduces melodiously. Nothing remains stable in this whirlpool of passions. Themes are torn to pieces, modulations are confused. The close inverts the beginning. Though the slow movement calms the tempo somewhat, it does not diminish the breadth of expression. The melody is interrupted by gloomy chords; pointed cries of despair and (a thing unheard of according to the rules of harmony then prevailing) wild calls release themselves in an unrelated key. Ghostlike, the third and fourth movement follow this. Hammering themes play at hide and seek, calmed by a short waltz rapture in the trio. The orchestration throughout the angrily breathing last movement is inimitable. The chase goes on till the very caricature of breathlessness is reached. And still it remains music up to the value of the highest three-barred note and the shortest rest.

The string quartet for two violins, viola and two

'celli takes us a step further in orchestration though not in musical excellence. Tradition has it that music has its most intense and noblest expression in the four part setting. Five parts are already an exception and a luxury. While the Middle Ages found expression in five parts we, today, express ourselves in four. This four-part distribution brings the greatest variety and opens up the greatest possibilities of instrûmentation and treatment of the different parts. All the more admirable is the masterly way in which Schubert conducts the five parts of his strings, acting as he does with such instinctive knowledge of the tone and the combination that there are no "empty" spots anywhere. The merry round of the instruments that carry the tune and of those that accompany it give infinite delight the more one analyses. In this tone picture there is a rising, a subduing, an ornamenting, an imitating, a waiting, a meeting in the *unisono* or in the many-voiced ensemble carried in such a manner that all the five voices are necessarily included in the whole. There are no repetitions or padding; everything is seen and found in five-fold manner at the very first glance. In the wonderful Adagio which is written in 12/8 time, broad and genial and rich with sentiment, one hears the first theme placed between ornamental voices by the second violin and the viola. One also hears the second theme with its upward motion carried by the first violin and the first 'cello. These are like colored ribbons in this incredibly delicately engraved ornamentation of voices. The first movement signifies labor; a landscape of peace is the meaning of the second; hurlyburly of the third, interrupted this time by a strangely slow trio; handicraft of the fourth with a Magyar, semi-Slavic coloring, a precious imitation of singing voices, a reflection of various keys, untrammeled expression of a hand sure of its touch. Play for the sake of play. The C Major Quintet was hidden for twenty-two years till men turned to practice it again.

The fate which the octet experienced was scarcely a better one. It was written for Count Troyer, who was an amateur player of the clarinet; and the famous Schuppanzigh played the first violin. The latter gave it another public performance after which it slumbered until 1861 when Hellmesberger produced it as a novelty. Schubert has used the wind instruments only on rare occasions in his chamber music. Here he added to a quintet of strings the clarinet in B Flat, the English horn in F, and the bassoon. He succeeded in writing a piece of much graver character than Beethoven's

Septet. A slow introduction advances, groaning under the weight of themes which are developed further. The pointed rhythm is the feature of the first movement; it is pressed from above, while it is drawn downwards in suspensions of the sixth, of the octave. There is a broad-meshed net of measures and melodic figures which fade away in the retarded echo of the horn. The slow theme is given to the clarinet which has a leading position almost throughout the entire movement, relieved only now and then by the first violin in combination with the horn, while the contribution of the bassoon remains limited. The Scherzo releases all the arts of orchestration while giving new strength to the age-old pointed rhythms. Once more, we have a movement of variations which provides all the instruments, even the contrabass, with the desired opportunity for a display of skill. That makes four movements. This piece is almost too complete; we are still to hear a Minuet as a mental recreation, and a sixth movement awaits us, which, this time, is not permitted to degenerate into a rondo or a potpourri of dances, but keeps a dignified and altogether serious attitude. There is a slow introduction full of expectations, a lively allegro play of closely adjusted motives in a hundred positions, repetitions, inversions. And then the Andante once more raises its warning finger, the Allegro hastens on towards its concert-like close, and the little symphony of eight instruments has run the gamut of every style and measure. The circle of Schubert's chamber music is closed. We are confronted by the orchestra.

SYMPHONIES

WHAT is Schubert's attitude to the symphony? Up to the present, we have become acquainted with him as the master of short forms of composition or of a few instruments. The compositions for orchestra seem to demand a larger scale. In his time the symphony was already the most imposing form of expression of absolute music, a confession of inner life, bearing witness to emotional depths. How had this form been developed? Its roots lay in the rationalism of the eighteenth century which imposed its severe tenets particularly on the first movement. The melody had been crystallized into the *motive*. There were a first and a second theme; sometimes a third and a fourth as well. These were related to one another in different keys. Then came the development, which placed the themes in counterpointed contrast to one another or analyzed them. Such an arrangement was the unalterable, logical one of an organism which dealt with definite themes, definite range of key and definite construction. Schubert remained bound by it. His romantic longing could only affect the vitalizing of the melodic and the harmonic material; he

might fondle the rhythm in folk-song fashion, see
that the development did not become too pedantic
or cling too closely to the repetition of the key;
but he could not change the system. It remained
in active force during the whole romantic period.
It was not overthrown until the time of Liszt's
Symphonic Poems; today the symphony permits
every kind of improvisation, the use of the rondo
form, in fact any kind of musical liberty. The less
the content approaches absolute music, the more
it defines and describes, the sooner the rigid construction gives way to psychological treatment.

The four movements of the symphony were the
remains of the suite. These also were "placed" by
psychology. At any rate, they provided the coming
romantic composer with the opportunity of shaping his work in a more graceful style without an
all too rigid adhesion to established forms. Thus
Schubert took the symphony the way he took the
sonata—as he found it. He never struggled with
the form; at the most he merely calmed it with
quiet. He never piled up weighty problems, but
let the music go on, no matter whether there are
few or many instruments. Nor did he have any
difficulties as far as *timbre* was concerned; because
he already possessed the skill of the romantic composer, departing from the sweetnesses of Mozart
and the urging unrest of Beethoven. His ensemble

sounds smooth and at peace with itself and is written with a knowledge of the *tutti* effects, no less than with a love of the solo instrument, without economy and yet without excess.

In any case, Schubert wrote the greater part of his symphonies in youth, stimulated by the amateur orchestra which he had at his disposal and where he had to limit himself in the orchestration, particularly with the brasses and the drums. These early symphonies are easy exercises whose musical value is continually increasing. Later he expressed himself more intensively in chamber music and let the orchestra rest for a while, the more since he scarcely had an opportunity to hear one of his symphonies performed. At the end of his life come the two great symphonies, the B Minor and the C Major, his most wonderful creations, which he himself never heard, and which remained buried until they were rediscovered to the general amazement. Altogether there are, if one counts the lost Gastein Symphony, nine symphonies; and, as in the case of Beethoven, of Bruckner, and of Mahler, the ninth, the last gift of the Muse, is the finale before the tomb.

Schubert was sixteen when he wrote the first of his symphonies. The convent orchestra played it for him. It is in the good old style filled with melody and gaiety. If one is forced to find something extraordinary in it, it might be the transition to the repetition in the first part which is set so beautifully over harmonies of wind instruments and is full of mysterious transpositions in long-drawn-out voices.

37. SYMPHONY II, PRESTO

37. Symphonie II Presto

In 1815 he wrote the Second Symphony. Here we have a slower introduction which gives it a somewhat graver appearance. And one notices in the repetition that peculiarity of Schubert's, the changing the key of the first theme: it is in E Flat instead of in B Flat. Schubert likes to give himself a free rein in these places, particularly where he takes the first theme up again. These are slight revolts, so to speak, against the law, which is never upset by a real revolution. Theme remains theme and construction, construction. How happy Schubert would have been if he had been allowed to find and formulate rules for himself. But, we can imagine him saying "one can manage this way, too." The old vase was large enough to contain all the flowers which he had for it. How gorgeous is the last movement of this symphony! This is no longer the rhythm of the rococo period; this is the folk-rhythm which Schubert so loves to re-introduce into musical composition. This measure, the fourth with the two-eighths, is given all possible opportunities in its motion, repetition and variation; nor did he ever improve on it.

Composed immediately after the second, the Third Symphony also has the slow introduction which suggests more weight than it has in reality. If one looks at the orchestration, one finds that it is not yet very personal. The themes are not

Schubert, from a pencil sketch on plaster of Paris, by Moritz von
Schwind, 1870

Program of Schubert's concert (1828) in the Society of the Friends of Music

grounded in the *timbre* itself, but transferred now to the woodwinds, now to the strings, always in a pleasing alternation and adjusted to the instrument which plays them. But how pretty is the invention, for instance, of the allegretto theme in the second movement, first sung by the strings and then given to the woodwinds in a dancelike rhythm. This symphony has little of lyrical restfulness. The last movement, a *presto vivace,* rushes on with the beat of a tarantella, throwing the chords and figures wildly topsy-turvy—F Sharp Minor, F Major, closely allied chords of surprising colorfulness.

The Fourth Symphony, written in 1816, Schubert called "the tragic symphony." The content, however, is not quite as serious as that. Though it may be a bit more grave than the preceding symphonies, it is after all thoroughly Schubertian in spirit, and remains a lyric play. It is written in C Minor, which may account for the comparison with Beethoven. But these two should never be compared. They inhabit two quite different regions; one, where speech bursts impetuously from the music, the other where it becomes more intimate in the guise of song or dance. The first and the last movements of this symphony possess a common bustling volubility and are similar in character. It is the lightly flowing play of unproblematic themes.

38. SYMPHONY IV, ANDANTE

38. Symphonie IV Andante

The chief joy lies in the slow movement. In this Andante there is apparent a depth and expansion which is significant of Schubert's emotional progress. It is not so much in the simple, singing first theme which the strings later alternate with the horns. More important is the next division, which begins with the sixteenths in F Minor and projects one of those broad asides which we find so often inserted in the slow movements, but then clings to a definite closing motive of descending suspensions, and spins this out in descending thirds, through violins, horns, clarinets, and flutes, so sweetly that the soul must stand and listen. Nor is this enough. Borne by flutes and clarinets, a second melodious turn is added which ascends and descends with incredible delicacy on lightly rounded basses. This is repeated in alternation and in succession. It is so exquisite (almost like a modern Russian melody), so melancholy and moving, that the mind refuses to relinquish it. If for no other reason, then for the sake of this movement alone, this symphony should be performed more frequently.

The Fifth Symphony (also dating from the year 1816) is orchestrated quite simply for an amateur orchestra without trumpets or drums, and, strange to say, is more remarkable because of its third and fourth movements than because of its first and second movements. The Minuet possesses a signal freshness of invention and liveliness in its interwoven parts. The last movement is a *vivace* of boundless merriment, melodically lovely, harmonically astonishing, and rhythmically in that ecstatic mood which emanated from Schubert in his best moments.

The Sixth Symphony dates from the next year. This time the third movement is designated as a Scherzo. The Minuet has no place in this movement. The symphony is somewhat meager in composition. It was intended for a small orchestra. It represents, so to speak, the symphonic calm before the breaking storm. There came a long pause in the making of symphonies while Schubert sharpened his wits with chamber music, and only in 1822 do we find him again busy with an important symphonic piece; a year before he had sketched an E Major symphony but had not finished it.

39. SYMPHONY IN B MINOR, FIRST MOVEMENT, G MAJOR THEME

39. Symphonie H=Moll. Erster Satz. G=Dur=Thema

Violoncello

pp

The great work of 1822 is the B Minor Symphony which has become famous as the "Unfinished" Symphony. Again we are faced by the question as to the completeness or incompleteness of certain of Schubert's works. We have already quieted ourselves by stating that certain pieces having six movements are over-complete, while this piece, with its two movements that were deemed sufficient by the composer, is surely no less complete and "finished." But a certain fact gives us pause: we possess a sketch for a third movement carried on through the scherzo and trio, even though not for all the parts and instruments. Did Schubert wish to go on with the piece and did he abandon it because he lacked the inclination to do so? Or did he leave it because he was dissatisfied to continue it in this manner? Only the gods can answer that. In the end, he abandoned the whole symphony, for no one except Anselm Hüttenbrenner knew anything of it and it was only discovered in 1865 by Herbeck among the latter's papers. Be that as it may, let us rejoice that we have at least these two movements which, in our judgment, are better and more finished in their construction than any possible third movement.

The B Minor Symphony begins, like so many others of Schubert's, with a theme played in unison. Here it is played as a mysterious pianissimo in the lower range by the 'celli and the basses. Then the violins add an accompanying figure in sixteenths, like the gurgle of water or the rustle of leaves. Already there is a hint of pastoral background in the music. To the accompaniment of the sixteenths in a comforting rhythm, a melody is pronounced by oboes and clarinets, not a continuance of the first mysterious theme, but a song of "linkèd sweetness long drawn out," carried to the treble, seconded by English horns and bassoons till a close is reached in B Minor. Here is pure lyricism. One thought follows the other, unfolding in succession rather than developing one from the other. To a syncopated accompanying figure of clarinets and bass viols, the 'cello begins the second theme, that cradling air in G Major which, though written within a range of five notes, is so rich in beauty that it has come to be the most famous melody in the world. Rising from the manuscript hidden away for forty-three years, it has spread abroad until it has become an intimate possession of every soul. Schubert delights in this melody. He immediately raises it one octave, lets the violins take it up and send it down to the octave below; and this rise and fall causes more exquisite pleasure than any other treatment. He breaks off. Complete silence for one measure. Heavy chords and then *tremoli* in C Minor, G Minor, and E Flat Major; the last is carried onward through a development of the third measure of the second theme until it passes away in the direction of G Major. Again a shaking up. Again a repetition. The theme recurs, treated by violins and flutes (this time pronouncing the first two measures) until B is finally reached. It is clear that Schubert treats this theme, which is melody itself, as pure music, as nothing but sounds which one may play with, may invert and marshal against one another. We have come to the frontiers of that period in which sounds were not only the material of music but the material of the spirit.

In this manner Schubert treats the first theme with which the symphony begins in the mysterious basses. We have not heard it again since the preamble. Now it reappears at the beginning of the second part. And what does he make of it? After the basses have given it another hearing, its first measures ascend in the violins above the weird tremolo of a low C in an incredibly moving lamentation covered by a longing suspension. It is carried on in this strain until it breaks out in a great outcry of pain which fades away in drooping chords. Theme has become emotion but emotion is converted into theme. The whole orchestra takes it up with full strength and turns it over in counterpoint through rolling runs, through pointed beats till the clouds are dispersed. The fog lifts, and the clear landscape of the opening is disclosed. The entire lyrical section is repeated. Then the mysterious motive again steps forward. It weaves its own entanglement, it builds up longing, it mourns toward a close in the woodwinds, violins and basses.

40. SYMPHONY IN B MINOR, SECOND MOVEMENT, C SHARP MINOR THEME

40. Symphonie H=Moll. Zweiter Satz. Cis=Moll=Thema

The second movement, the Andante con moto, begins as if nothing had ever existed—dawn of the world; clear chords in horns and bassoons; melodic ascent of violins; a three-eighths measure which moves without definite accent. An outburst of a seventh chord follows; chromatically united with it, a cluster of sevenths shines forth. Instruments alternate with one another in soft chords, in runs on the octave; sevenths glisten, melodies twinkle; the line grows tenser, becomes articulate, a sonant mirror. The violin takes up G Sharp and lets it descend to C Sharp Minor. The strings syncopate an accompaniment. The clarinet raises its voice in simple thirds, singing a melody of such moving sadness, so broadly, so intensely that the violins tremble (lightly bowing over the dominant) and seem to weep. The middle voices descend, vary enharmonically, until the tune of the clarinets becomes more and more spiritual and they wander back to C Sharp, passing through the circle of harmonies. Everything is so permeated with melody that the instruments seem to utter their song as if from human lips and the voices in their eternal questioning and answering seek the Infinite through music. This is clear magic. An oboe in D Flat Major begins the melody in thirds, while the 'cello plays around it, letting the melody glide downward from the heights over tonic and dominant into an appealingly simple figure, chaste and direct in its sentiment. Then the flute begins and the oboe softly replies as in a dream, a response which the other instruments try to emulate. But we know our Schubert. Here, as elsewhere, what was soul becomes *motive*. In the unison of full orchestra the bass picks up the theme of the clarinets and conducts it over the other parts through a set of figures, as though it were a kind of formal theme subject to development. But the lyric note prevails and gladly returns. Though the rule required slow movements to contain such *tutti* outbursts, it was none the less possible to interweave and entwine thematic parts gracefully in lyrical mood and measure. Now the time has come to return to the beginning. Changed in keys, the same story begins all over again, more emphatic in the regulation of counterpoint, where there is room for a large gesture. In the finale we have again the delicate gesture shaping the phrase with lyrical tenderness—unaccompanied strains of the violins; interspersed among them, chords of the woodwinds in unrelated keys; a lovely flashing of the figure in sevenths; descent and the last low breath.

41. THE "GREAT" SYMPHONY IN C MAJOR, FIRST MOVEMENT

41. Symphonie C=Dur (große). Erster Saß

The C Major Symphony written in 1828 was lost to the world for ten years. Schumann found it in 1838 through Ferdinand Schubert. It was performed for the first time in 1839 by Mendelssohn at a concert in the Gewandhaus in Leipzig. This composer may have found many of its features related to his own work. One would like to go on saying "This is Schubert's finest piece of work," but, to be candid, one can never decide which is the most beautiful. At any rate, in none of the other pieces can we remark so definitely how easily he produces, against the background of his invention, new ideas without laboring over them; how each new idea helps to give birth to another; how the whole represents a beautifully ordered structure.

[168]

Here, too, he begins with a theme recited by solo instruments, in this instance, the horns. The theme has a romantic woodland strain, virile and proud, and so varied in its rhythm that it might have become a patriotic hymn. It forms the slow introduction to the first movement. The horns give this theme to the woodwinds, which harmonize it beautifully while the violins accompany. In the third repetition, the trombones join the chorus as the theme displays its full force. The orchestra becomes excited. The motive is the root of every kind of heroism. Once again it sounds in the woodwinds, over the strings, climbs higher, circles the dominant, and is shaken in every fibre of its being until it paves the way for the actual first theme of the presto movement which follows at once. This is a theme full of dancing rhythms. Beethoven would have shaped it into something heroic; Schubert gives it a free-swinging, easy motion. This swinging and sliding continues uniformly. It trembles in attuned chords. It is revived in the happy turn of a cadence. In broad triplets in four-fourths time, it sweeps up and down in the scale of G Major. A godlike, untroubled soaring, a gentle lassitude of power. The triplet of the four-quarters measure penetrates the two-part beat, until it rests on a C, and glides over B into E minor. The second theme makes its appearance in oboes and bassoons, later

in flutes and clarinets. Here again we have a dancing and gliding, with a mocking motion from high
to low and back again to high. This mockery is
carried on with a teasing accentuation, through all
the keys, through the entire range of voices till
nothing is left but the rocking of chords which
spreads through the whole orchestra. Here we have
the first sounds of that romantic mood which meets
us in Mendelssohn's *Meeresfluten,* in Wagner's
Feuerzauber. And at this point, as if in expectation
of further development, middle parts are audible
in the orchestra, like the voices of ghosts. The
trombones sound them, they are a transposition of
the first theme of the introduction. The calls become more urgent, they aim towards the G, a memory of the second theme. This part closes on the
dominant. In the development, everything that
has gone before is inverted. The first and the second allegro themes approach one another. The diatonic scales are interwoven with them. The triplet
gleams through the rhythm. The trombones interrupt with the solemnity of the andante theme.
Gradually the tangled web is unwound. The andante motive is carried through woodwinds and the
lower strings. The triplets bring on the repetition
of the allegro. And the delightful play begins again
in altered keys and with the *stretta* of the *finale,*
which expands the orchestra by broadly swelling

House in which Schubert died, Kettenbruckengasse, Vienna

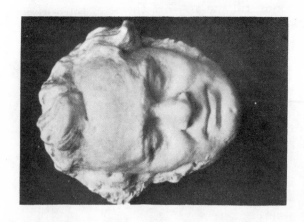

Death masks of Schubert

chords and diatonic ascents, rising like the breath
of the cosmos, till the andante theme again unites
all the instruments with solemnity and leads them
onward to a close in the affirmative key of C Major.

42. THE "GREAT" SYMPHONY IN C MAJOR, SECOND MOVEMENT (THEME)

42. Symphonie C-Dur (große). Zweiter Satz (Thema)

The quintet of strings plays in quiet eighths. The
basses give the first intimation of a rhythm which
has a popular strain, a slightly Slavic mournfulness.
A bit Hungarian, perhaps, for the two approach
each other. To this accompaniment, the oboe brings
the theme, a theme famous for its spiritual expression, a theme that seems to contemplate itself. The
clarinets join in. The theme moves from A Minor,
with a Schubertian pianissimo, into A Major and
reveals its sentimental and German soulfulness. The
strings rejoice in a romantic dance, in rocking
basses and pointed melodies. Now they call on the
clarinets and the bassoon to take their turn. One
never grows weary with the repetitions; there is so
much charm in this enchanting music. And again
one returns to the first theme on by-paths while

the woodwinds have their opportunity, now A
Minor now A Major. One cannot hear it too often.
A new motive makes itself felt; the key changes
to F Major. The strings carry it up and down
diatonically. The clarinets rejoice in the song; the
flutes join them. But not content with this fulness
of melody, the theme starts again in F Major and
is developed with such enchanting polyphony that
there are few passages in music so rich in sweetness. But no, there is more to come. The clarinet
lifts a plaintive yearning to the accompaniment of
a rocking bass in D Minor. The horns interrupt
with calls of the previous motive. There is deep
calm. Chords take deep breaths. We are back at
the beginning of the movement; the A Minor
melody begins again with a livelier orchestra, and
the whole circle of melodies is reviewed again. Then
the strings grow tenser and a conflict threatens;
but the pulses are quieted. The 'cello sings a new
tune of mournful beauty; the oboe takes it up,
and the harmonies are changed to A Major. In this
key, the singing second theme is developed with
more movement, more breadth and more breath;
an infinite self-satisfaction until we reach the A
Minor theme for the third time and hear this sing
itself to sleep. Who could complain that it is too
much?

The Scherzo is a hide-and-seek of two rhythms through the orchestra: six headlong eighths and three headlong fourths. They rush through the varying harmonies. The voice of a violin sings a graceful peasant melody over the accompaniment. The woodwinds unite and intune a rustic waltz with all those little impertinences of transitions which Schubert loved to use. Yet broad and sonorous chords are not lacking. Sometimes they remind one of the first movement, but the tittering of the main rhythm predominates and permeates the whole movement; kicks up its heels with indescribable agility. The trio, in contrast, moves in a more solid sphere. It is the perfect romantic song in A Major; in it is all the longing, all the ascending emphasis, all the melody and rhythm of a chorus for male voices. How broadly it is spread. How its measures are stretched over periods of time. Schubert allows it to extend itself. Not because he does not know how to make an ending to his piece, but rather because his desire demands wide spaces. He is the musician of volume. He fills it with all the happiness of his inspiration.

The finale is a ferment. It is an orgy of figures and cadences. Half-notes beat the ground. Triplets whirl. Notes collide. Melodies are lifted up like snapping flags. All thematic material is merged

[173]

in this carnival. Diatonic scales are transformed into runs, sustained by pointed basses. Between them, horns sound their joy. The first theme is characterized by a steady stream of running triplets; the second by beats, then by triplets. The beats and scales are carried thematically through the whole orchestra which riots in new formations. A diatonic motive descends through all the instruments before the close of the first division. At the opening of the second, it becomes a melody accompanied by basses and makes an attempt at development by joining the theme of the four drum beats, rushing through the different harmonies, sustained by a tremendous organ point in G. Now it aims to attain the beginning again, but, instead of ascending to G, it descends to E Flat. E Flat Major starts a commotion. The motives are carried through all the related keys; there is no peace; triplets, beats, follow rapidly. We seem to be tracing the steps of the repetition when a rumbling of basses penetrates a very underbrush of keys; the notes cry out, crowd and push one another, the motive of the four drum beats reaches the pitch of mad exuberance which a few treble melodies vainly try to calm. The wild spirits are brought to earth in a deep C. The last symphony is ended. What would the next have been? This is the dance of death:

GREAT SYMPHONY C MAJOR, LAST MOVEMENT
43. Symphonie C=Dur (große). Letzter Satz

THE REST

THERE remain the larger compositions for the voice (principally the choral works both for male and female voices, the pieces for mixed chorus), the religious compositions, among which the masses come foremost, and finally the operas. From these compositions, which represent a major part of Schubert's life-work, or, at all events, the longest period of working time, only a few of the choral works have survived. Schubert, whose special grace was intimacy, was less at home in works of extended volume. Notwithstanding, we must not neglect mentioning them, because such pieces show the utmost limit of Schubert's sphere of activity, though it seems that his real character diminishes in shape and form in these broad spaces.

From the group of choral works for male voices, which at that time were written for musical entertainment rather than as an expression of lofty art, we may pick out several noteworthy compositions. The most important is Goethe's "Gesang der Geister über den Wassern" (Song of the Spirits over the Water), a poem which so attracted Schubert that he was tempted to give it new form, over and over again. First he tried it as a simple song, then he wrote it for male voices without accompaniment, again with piano accompaniment. Finally, in February, 1821, he gave it the present form, a most exceptional one. The text is sung by four tenor and four bass voices. The accompaniment is executed by low strings only, two violas, two 'celli and the contrabasses. The gloomy and mysterious atmosphere is expressed in the instruments used.

44. SONG OF THE SPIRITS OVER THE WATER, CHORUS FOR MALE VOICES

44. Gesang der Geister über den Wassern. Männerchor

The contrabasses play pianissimo the well-known Schubert rhythm of one quarter-note with two eighth-notes. The other strings weave a mysterious introduction over this. All eight voices intone

the text: "the soul of man is likened to the water."
All begin on C but soon the parts are divided. This
occurs at the words: "it comes from heaven."
Tenors and basses alternate. Where the text reads:
"it ascends again to heaven," the voices unite and
ascend fortissimo. Just as in his songs, Schubert
again depicts first mood then textual contents and,
finally, unites both into a ringing unity. At the
words: "it must descend to earth again," tenors
and basses take the text from one another in alternately descending lines. At the line "ever changing," the voices for the first time assume a richer
polyphonic character to denote this change. The
orchestra accentuates the various divisions. The
pure stream drops from high steep rocks; the basses
receive it in unison. It rises in cloudy cascades as
the tenors take it up again and the theme is depicted in gracefully sinking and rising chords, ornamented by flourishes of the strings. We remain
in the same picture as softly rustling veils are
painted by tenors and basses, now in imitation of,
now in opposition to one another. Then steep cliffs
break the fall of the water. The movement grows
livelier. Basses and tenors raise their voices in octaves in divided parts, till, summoned by the basses,
the entire sea of voices breaks against the cliffs.
The foam rushes in sixteenth-notes through the

basses, both in the voices and in the instruments, enclosed by the chords of the tenors. How like an angry outburst in an old oratorio! Schubert is tempted to develop this stormy middle section. He allows the themes to drop swiftly down through the score, always retaining the contrast of rolling sixteenths and rhythmic chords until both are lost in the abyss, while the contrabass hums a repetition. Now the scene opens on a cheerful, watered valley. Water, described by Schubert in such varied terms, shapes more melodious contours, and the planets mirror their countenances in the infinite peacefulness of softly splashing musical figures. The wind blows up, a winning fellow, not a storm. He strokes the melody to rest. We have come back to the beginning. In the first rhythm, in the old chords, man's soul is compared to the water, man's fate to the wind. In the quiet alternation of F Minor and C Major the music sinks to earth. This is a beautiful composition, neat in structure as it is rich in content. At the time it was composed it excited the hearers by the boldness of its modulations. Today it is considered a classic.

The "Nachtgesang in Walde" (Nightsong in the Forest) has always held an exceptional position among choral works for male voices. Nothing more

German can be conceived. The orchestra consists of four horns, the voices demand two tenors and two basses. Though one calls this a chorus it may as well be called four solo parts. The horns play the introduction; romantic voices of night in the forest; the voices welcome the night, losing themselves entirely in melody. The horns answer the voices and sustain them. As rustling winds arise, the scene becomes more picturesque. The voices remain in accord, they call out of their sleep, they challenge the horns. The horns grow livelier and intone the accompaniment, so characteristic of Schubert, the quarter-note with the eighths. And the voices, always joined, a veritable choral union, ascend from the pianissimo to the forte and call the night to come out of the forest; the charming night, which they apostrophize in graceful figure work. Perhaps this goes a little beyond the limits of the noblest artistic expression; perhaps it smacks a bit of the singing society. But may we be struck dead on the spot, if there is not always a bit of this sentimentality in our good Schubert!

There is no gainsaying that "Die Hymne" (The Hymn) written in October, 1828, is much more important. Again the accompaniment has extraordinary character. There are no strings whatsoever; only oboes, clarinets, bassoons, trumpets, horns and trombones. Two tenors and two basses have solo parts; two tenors and two basses form a chorus. But the style of the composition is entirely adapted to the general public. The soloists begin without accompaniment with a hymn-like section which gradually permits the different parts a definite place in the structural development. Following this, the chorus chants the same melody and is accompanied in counterpoint most effectively by the solo voices. The second section is managed by the chorus in psalmodic style, but eventually this chorus returns to the hymn-like melody of the beginning and lets the soloists participate. The close is formal and repeats the first section exactly. In such matters Schubert clings closely to the general style of contemporaneous choral composition, and only now and then a charming melodic outgrowth or a delicate modulation, as for instance from the C Major of the chorus to the A Major of the soloists, reveals his authorship.

Among the songs for male voices with piano accompaniment, we should mention "Der Gondelfahrer" (The Gondolier) based on the text of Mayrhofer's poem. With all Schubertian suppleness, two tenors and two basses sing their serenade in gay and friendly fashion to a swinging accompaniment.

45. THE LITTLE VILLAGE, CHORUS FOR
MALE VOICES

45. Das Dörfchen. Männerchor

Then we have "Das Dörfchen" (The Little Village), based on Bürger's poem, which even at that time was among the most popular compositions for male chorus. Instead of the piano accompaniment he added an accompaniment for guitars. Two tenors and two basses begin to praise their village in a simple romantic tune which is delightfully constructed. At the lines "where the hawthorns blossom" they become more reflective in tone and the different parts are more clearly defined, the voices trying out different passages requiring skill. Then the canon commences. The first tenor begins it on the word "happiness," with a gay student's strain; the other voices follow in the stipulated order, while the first voices continue their song. Thus this romantic story of the village is interwoven with many pretty touches of artistic skill which do honor to our master's craftsmanship.

No other Schubert chorus for female voices is as famous as "Das Ständchen" (Serenade). In its present form it is written for a contralto solo voice and a chorus of two sopranos and two altos. The piano supplies the plucking guitarlike accompaniment, which, with slight variations, is kept up throughout the whole piece. The manner in which the solo voice challenges the chorus, while the chorus answers hesitatingly, is indescribably graceful. Both become more and more bold in melody,

[183]

inspiring one another; they play at hide and seek; the chorus develops its fugue; the solo is incorporated into it; the harmonies alternate with one another delicately and lightly; all so laughing, light-footed and playful, so breathlessly musical, so tender that it vanishes as quickly as an evanescent odor.

In speaking of the "Ständchen" one ought always to tell the pleasant story which was handed down to us by Anna Fröhlich. "Every time that the name-day or the birthday of the Gosmar girl (one of her pupils) approached, I used to go to Grillparzer and ask him to write something for the occasion. And so when her birthday came again, I went, as usual, to him and said: 'Well, my dear Grillparzer, there's nothing for it; you must write me a poem again for the Gosmar's birthday.' He replied: 'Gladly, if something occurs to me.' Says I to him, 'Well, you had better see to it that something *does* occur to you.' In a few days he gave me the 'Serenade,' 'with bent finger I knock gently—.'" Later, when Schubert came to see us, I said to him; 'See here, Schubert, you have got to write the music to that for me.' Says he, 'let's see' and, leaning against the piano, he cried out over and over again: 'My, how fine that is. That's really beautiful.' He studied the page a while and then he said: 'There you are, it is practically finished, I have it already.'

46. SERENADE, CHORUS FOR FEMALE VOICES

46. Ständchen. Frauenchor

And actually in three days he brought it to me finished; for a mezzo-soprano (for Pepi in fact) and four male voices. Then I said to him, 'No, Schubert, I cannot use it this form; it is intended as an ovation to Gosmar from her girl friends. You must rewrite that chorus for female voices.' I well remember just what I said to him, as he sat there, by the window. Soon afterwards he brought it to me in its present form, for Pepi's voice and the female chorus. I had my pupils brought to Döbling in three carriages. The Gosmar girl lived there in the little Lang House. The piano had been hidden under her windows in the garden and Schubert had been invited. He did not come, however. The next day when I asked him why he had been absent, he excused himself, 'Oh, yes, I forgot about it entirely.' Then I had the Ständchen performed publicly in the Hall of the Musical Society in the Tuchlauben and had urged him repeatedly to be present. We were about to begin, but our dear Schubert was still missing. Dr. Jenger and Walcher, later councillor of the archduke, were present. When I told the latter that I was really inconsolable that Schubert should again miss the performance, since he had never heard the Serenade performed, and that I wondered where he had hidden himself this time, Walcher conceived the brilliant idea of looking for him at the inn 'Zur Eiche'

(The Oaktree) in the Brandstätte. Musicians liked to go there because the beer was so good. Sure enough, there he was, and Walcher fetched him to the concert hall. After the performance Schubert was in raptures and said to me: 'Really, I did not think that it could be as beautiful as that.' "

Considering Schubert's works for mixed chorus one must pause at "Lazarus." This is an oratorio based on a German text, in three parts, written for Resurrection Day. It has, however, been left in fragmentary form. It was indeed a strange undertaking to write music which is not divided into definite sections for a text which has a certain dramatic structure. But Schubert succeeds here no better than in his operas in establishing our contact with his *dramatis personæ*, lost, as many of them are, in monotonous passages. There are certain moods, expressing the sadness of life and of nature, which remind one of Parsifal. The text says: "Swooning Nature is overcome, and yet it must bear its pain, though it would willingly give back to the Creator this life of sorrows, as it sighs and struggles toward extinguishment." The music which Schubert has written to these lines possesses wonderful melancholy in its slowly breathing rhythm.

Although the masses which Schubert wrote are really for mixed chorus, they must be considered as official church music. To be frank, this type of music was not, by reason of temperament, his special predilection. However, it was the task of the professional musician to do his share for the Church. Bach did it by creating a system of metaphysics which creates a heaven on earth. Beethoven fought out his personal struggles in his masses and depicted the landscape and background of the celestial kingdom rather than a pious ecstasy. Schubert is confronted with none of these problems. He writes the masses with a feeling for the power of music which speaks to us in pure form, without mystical devotion or Italian worldliness. He bases them on proven principles and here and there he seizes an opportunity to show his picturesqueness, his harmonic boldness and his melodic charm.

There exist six masses written by him. The first four are simple and unassuming in structure. The fifth is enhanced both in method and quality. The sixth, in E Flat Major, was written just a few months before his death. It marks a climax. Let us observe it closely so that we may judge of the style of this church music. The choir is divided into four parts, the traditional arrangement, and there are four or five soloists. The orchestra calls for no flutes, an omission noticeable in similar compositions by Schubert, but the organ, which the fifth

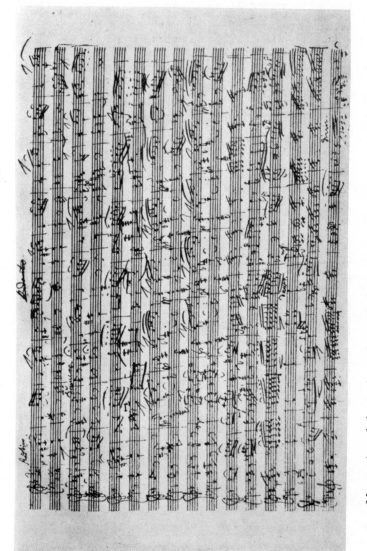

Manuscript of the Andante from Schubert's Piano Sonata, E Flat Major, Op. 122

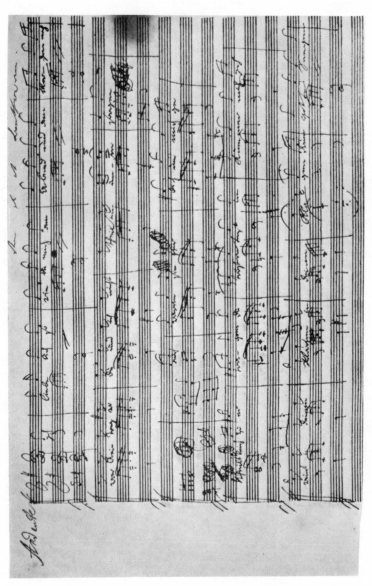

Beethoven's "Ich Liebe Dich" on the reverse side of Schubert's manuscript

mass still retains, is missing as well. To a quintet of strings he adds two oboes, two clarinets, two bassoons, two horns, two trombones, and later kettledrums and trumpets.

The *Kyrie* is given to the orchestra in slowly creeping chords supported by the sustained rhythms. The chorus sings the "appeal for pity" *pianissimo*. Soft melodic lines awake in the woodwinds and in the sopranos. When the Savior is called, the ensemble rises to a *fortissimo* of loud horns, strings in tremolo and ringing basses. There is a return to the *Kyrie*, to the mysterious mood of the beginning, when the melodic lines, the polyphony of the middle voices expands in a renewed *fortissimo*. The movement closes with gentle chords.

The *Gloria* is sung impetuously, first by the unaccompanied choir, then joined by the rushing orchestra. "Peace on earth" is interspersed quietly. The "song of praise to God" carries the voices higher. At the "adoration" they descend, softly, mysteriously. *Gratias agimus tibi:* the first melody appears in the woodwinds to a *pizzicato* accompaniment of the strings, and the chorus supplies the harmonies. The isolation of the voices is still timidly maintained, until the *gloria* again receives the full burden of voices and instruments. Now comes the first dramatic convulsion. Trom-

47. Sechste Messe. Sanctus SIXTH MASS SANCTUS
Adagio

Sanc — — tus   Domi-nus Deus Sabaoth!

Sanc — — tus   Domi-nus Deus Sabaoth!

bones blow a liturgical theme while strings play in *tremolo*. The chorus cries out to God, to God who bears the sins of the universe. Terrified, even of self, it can only breathe out the *Miserere* in mournfully interwoven harmonies illuminated by woodwinds. The elements of both instruments and voices are splintered into such contrasts. *Cum sancto spiritu*: the bass begins a fugue-like theme, heavily and solemnly. Tenor, contralto and soprano build on it. The theme is expanded and tightened according to well established rules. Figures are enlaced, each echoing the other. The composition spreads out in infinite breadth; there is scarcely an interlude of the orchestra. The melodic lines grow shorter, the "Amen" is exhaled at the close.

The *Credo* begins with a roll of drums. The voices proclaim their faith in strong regular chords, intermingled with transparent fugati. It is time to return to the lyrical mood. The 'cello propounds a short Schubertian melody, broad and slow, in twelve-eighths time. The middle strings rock gently under it. The first tenor solo takes up his theme and, as it develops, hands it over to the second tenor solo. The soprano delights in it. It is the song of Christ's incarnation. The whole choir bears the crucifixion. Cruel chords, raised to the diminished seventh, join the trembling rhythms of the strings. Again the contrast is repeated. Drums roll and the chorus advances into a movement embodying the *Resurrexit*. This proves to be a majestic portrayal of unswerving belief. The *Credo* comes forward again. In the pure music of voices superimposed, one on the other, the "Amen" scarcely finds the way to the end.

The *Sanctus* sounds the climax. Schubert yields himself to all temerities or modulation: E Flat Major, B Minor, G Minor, E Flat Minor follow one another. In these summons the voices wax *fortissimo*. The heavens are filled with the praises of the Lord, the voices with polyphony. "Hosannah" is carried through all registers to the infinite glory of God, of music and of Schubert. A mighty hand has written these pages. As they become part of the soul of man, they bear witness to what Schubert could do with church music. Thus he imagined the Lord, thus he put Him into music.

The *Benedictus* is calm. The first violin dreams over a melody profound and sweet in tone. The four solo voices develop it with delicacy. The chorus interpolates a fugato. Soloists and chorus alternate thus throughout the section. It is apparent that Schubert longed to express himself only melodically in this movement. He adds the fugue of the *Hosannah* to it, as a concession to the demands of musical tradition.

The *Agnus Dei* is nearest to his heart. Its theme and mood have been compared to that of the "Doppelgänger." The rhythms tread heavily. The voices intertwine chromatically. Where he asks for peace, he inclines again to a graceful melodic contour. The soli supply light and shade, alternating more rapidly than usual with the tutti, until light and darkness approach one another in sharp contrasts. *Dona nobis pacem:* the last appeal to the Lord is a hymnlike cadence in *fortissimo* which evaporates on a breath in E Flat Major.

And the opera? Can one imagine that Schubert could ever have written an opera having a real popular success? A different temperament is required for that. The composer of an opera needs to be able to work in plot as well as in music for his effects. He adds the music to heighten or to intensify dramatic conflicts. An outburst of passions or an embodiment of contrasts is more important to him than all lyrical expression. His only justification for lyricism is that it may provide a reaction to the drama. Whatever has been thrown topsy-turvy, overemphasized or destroyed by the course of the action, is carried by the lyric to a quiet spot, where emotion may have its outlet. The

lyric mood helps music to fulfil the demands of
reminiscence and the inevitable reconciliation required at the end of opera. What interest had
Schubert in such problems? When he set a text to
music, such music was embellished by small tone-
pictures which arose from his innermost soul.
When he wrote symphonies or chamber music he
did not need any extra stimulation. For the musician of intimate feeling the opera brings only confusion. He finds himself and the purity of his
medium confronted by paradoxes which he can
scarcely overcome. His strength in absolute music
is such that never successfully will he subject it
to the conflicts of dramatic action. At most, he
may subdue such action to the laws of his own
delicate temperament, destroying thereby the very
essence of operatic composition. How attractive
this is when we can see it as strength not as weak-
ness.

Notwithstanding, Schubert (as a product of his
time and even more in the hope of large earnings)
embarked on this doubtful enterprise. He wrote,
or at least began, a large number of operas and
lyrical plays, of which scarcely a trace has come
down to us. He was uncritical in his judgment of
librettos, which were about the most stupid ever
offered to a composer. He took no pains whatsoever to arouse the dramatic sense in his hearers or

to further the "effects." The charming bits which still survive are happy accidents. Look at the very titles of the operas: "Des Teufels Lustschloss" (The Devil's Pleasure Palace), "Der vierjährige Posten" (Sentry for Four Years), "Fernando," "Die beiden Freunde von Salamanka" (The Two Friends of Salamanca), "Die Zwillingsbrüder" (The Twins), "Die Verschworenen oder der häusliche Krieg" (The Conspirators or the Domestic War), "Die Zauberharfe" (The Magic Harp), "Rosamunde von Zypern" (Rosamunde of Cyprus), "Alfonso und Estrella" (Alfonso and Estrella), "Fierrebras" (Fierrebras), a number of topical songs in other operas and a great many fragments. Can one understand the reason for so much waste energy? Most of them are not worth mention. I choose certain examples, giving details of some of the most typical.

"The Magic Harp" was performed twelve times. That was the most that could be expected of it. It contained a pretty overture (of which we shall speak again) and some charming melodramatic passages. Mottl tried to preserve this music by incorporating it into a version of Raimund's "Gefesselte Phantasie" (Imagination Enchained). "Alfonso and Estrella," after Liszt's attempt to revive it at Weimar, was taken up by others. But in vain. The impossible action of Schober's romantic fairy

play always killed it. Its dull length drags down
the music which is full of gay choirs, preludes
for the orchestra, sentimental airs, picturesque
sketches, ensembles for conspirators, ballads,
marches and finali. In "Fierrebras," it is even
worse. Schubert composed this opera for the finan-
cier Barbaja; and Josef Kupelwieser (brother of
the painter) wrote the libretto. It had just as few
performances as "Alfonso and Estrella." Though
it contains charming numbers for the chorus,
marches, romances, night-pieces and ensembles,
and though the orchestration is given particular
attention, this lavish invention is joined to a drama
which could move no one.

We may pause a bit longer with "Die Verschworenen" (The Conspirators). Of all Schubert's
operas, this has been performed the greatest number of times. The style of his music is best adapted
to a libretto which (as in this case) demands no
dramatic movement, but is content with a succession of tone pictures. In the year 1823 Ignatz
Franz Castelli supplied him with the libretto for
the one act play. Castelli published it in a volume of his "Dramatische Sträusschen" (Dramatic
Nosegays) and accompanied it with this state-
ment: "The complaint of the German composers
usually is: 'Yes, we would like to compose operas,
if you poets would only supply us with librettos.'

Here is one for you, gentlemen. If you wish to add music to it, I beg you allow my words to have some significance and do not destroy the meaning of the intrigue by preferring coloratura to musical characterization. I believe that opera should be dramatic action joined to music, not merely music based on a text. And the impression made by the whole seems to me more important than giving this or that singer an opportunity for vocal pyrotechnique. Let us do something for essentially German opera, gentlemen."

The censor changed the title "The Conspirators" as being too anarchistic, to "Häusliche Krieg" (Domestic War). Schubert gave himself heart and soul to the music. He really did write something which might be called "a German opera." He submitted it in Vienna and heard nothing further about it. A year later the manuscript was returned to him unread. In Berlin, too, nothing could be done, for there another composition having the same title had already been produced. The musical play was performed for the first time in Vienna, on March first, 1861, in a concert-hall. Castelli, then eighty years old, was present. When he was asked about Schubert, he said that he had known him in person, but he had been told that Schubert's composition was much too gloomy and entirely without humour and that, therefore, he had given the matter no further attention. In October, 1861, the Viennese Imperial Opera produced the piece. In the following year it was given in Munich by Schubert's friend, Lachner. At that time Schwind, the painter, wrote: "Schubert's little opera has made me quite happy. What simple and innocent pleasure there is in creating such beautiful music, what exuberance, and what feeling for dramatic effect! With a little more experience, he would have been the equal of Weber."

The contents of "The Conspirators" lent itself well to Schubert's style. It is the story of a revolt of the wives against their husbands, modelled on Lysistrata. The men are knights who have left their wives during the Crusades, a good opportunity for the use of male chorus. And the women who wish to be revenged on the men, by refusing them their caresses, afford the same opportunity for female choirs. Such groups may also unite in a mixed chorus. If you take a few soloists from among the men and the women, who are to give the action personal force and differentiation, you have your dramatic operatic ensemble according to the least complicated scheme. And the fact that, finally, the interplay of intrigue and ruse ends in a general reconciliation, is more in the direction of Schubert's bent than any unrelieved tragedy. All he had to do was to use his favorite types for the single musical numbers and he could satisfy completely his own requirements as well as those of the libretto. His whole repertory of songs, choral works and marches is brought into play and the symmetry of the dramatic action favors the adherence to all formal rules.

We have, for instance, the duet between the page and the Lady's-maid, the typical minor "comic relief." They recognize one another, are somewhat in doubt about their mutual feelings, and then embrace again. Nothing is easier than to arrange this action into a charming symmetry. They supply one another with the most charming Schubertian melodies; they repeat, with infinite pleasure, their vocal sweetness; and, finally, they unite in a popular duet, in which each of the voices has an equal part because each figure and phrase is allotted with impartial regularity. Close to this, is Helen's *romanza.* No one can doubt that this fine number in F Minor is a genuine gift of Schubert, who furnished it with all the delicate turns of altered transition notes in order to carry it, as he loved to do, into a gentle F Major. The ensemble that, soon afterwards, begins in C Major has as its basis one of those entrancing dancelike accompaniments out of which melodies rise of their own accord. The first chorus for female voices, which is pleasantly interrupted by the song of the countess, swings its harmonies sweetly throughout the movement. The rhythm changes to the measure of a polonaise (much favored by Schubert) and thereupon a romantic tune is developed which can scarcely be distinguished from Weber's work. Choir and soloists have an easy task to base their phrasing on it. F Major has become F Minor in which the melodious complaints occur, while the polonaise gives an undercurrent of power. The equipment is there for the more complicated form of the movement. The female chorus and all the soloists perform a pretty number in C Major, adding to the various voices of the ensemble a new dexterity, and running the gamut of Schubert's light melodiousness. Here we have the first important accomplishment. Its character is determined by Schubert rather than by the operatic style.

Later, there is another opportunity for women's chorus. The women swear they will be revenged. The countess has the solo part. We have thus the same combination of voices as before. But this is Schubert's special province. The end of the movement is also typical. The voices steal away, pianissimo, as in hundreds of other Italian or German operas. It is high time for the appearance of a male chorus. A fine march theme in B Minor introduces it. The knights celebrate peace with an overconfident and happy air in D Major, like a jolly student's song, gay and sure of success. Nor does the ensemble No. 6 show any great leaning towards pedantry. Though the page betrays the plan of the women to the men, for he has a female voice and was secretly present at the meeting of the conspiring wives, everything goes smoothly along the paths of the strophic song. A short melody is the foundation on which the count and the page sing their dialogue, the chorus providing the accents. On occasions when stormy action seems to be demanded, Schubert throws in a bold modulation and thereby gives the dramatic action what is its due. The ensemble gains in breadth. The count and the page, together with the chorus, consume a quantity of chords and set their voices gaily one against the other. The women are not to derive any benefit from their ruse. On the word "none" there is a striking rhythm alternating between song and orchestra, after which the conclusion is a simple matter.

Now the time has come to join the two choirs. First it is the turn of the women on a far-flung melody and then that of the men, somewhat less gentle in harmonic structure. The interspersed solo voices have quite a time and make a pretty impression. The women are endowed with a new theme faster and more excited in character, and, after the soli of the male voices have contributed their interlude, the male choir takes over this selfsame theme, in spite of the fact that this is wholly illogical. But Schubert paid more attention to the demands of the music than any demand of probability. Count and countess, though enemies, support the same melody through a duet written in the form of a canon. Now comes the clash. The knights begin a new melody in the manner of a drinking song, and the women in stressed chords oppose it, with astonished questions. But it would not be a true comic opera if the two choirs did not finally exchange their themes and repeat the whole main section as a musical exercise. Which is precisely what happens.

A duet between Astolf and Helen starts in with unaccustomed gloomy tones which, perhaps, have occasioned the reproach that Schubert was melancholy. The duet soon resolves into a flexible melody with all the chromatic shading characteristic of Schubert's idiom. It is sung first by him, then by her. As the orchestra grows more lively, they approach one another and, following the good old Italian example, change to an Allegro in which their voices are effectively contrasted according to approved methods and embellished with free harmonies. The arietta which the count sings has the same structure as one of Schubert's Lieder. The constantly repeated "for thee" has the effective accents of well-known refrains in the love-songs. It is a beautiful number, worthy of the master in the romantic suppleness of melodic and harmonic treatment and in the wonderful freedom of modulation, which follows every emotional change. It is quite in keeping with the style of this opera when the countess takes up the same air with another text and parodies it with the repeated refrain "for me."

Assuredly the finale will not bring us any dramatic surprises. Catastrophe and reconciliation are expressed in dancelike rhythms, chorus and solo assenting. A sustaining melody which was first sung by the orchestra is taken up by the countess. Suddenly, a brisk marching tune with a charming accent on the ninth note begins pianissimo, sung first by the countess, then repeated by the women in chorus. It is the song to which they are to march forth to battle. The small confusion which results is soon resolved into the dancing mood. The double choirs step forth. They reveal themselves in graceful counterplay of ensembles; the first tune descends on the finale; a charming male quartet continues the mood; the chorus of knights carries it further; and, under the benign influence of the first melody, the couples are reconciled in the drama, having already been reconciled for some time in the music. An air possessing idyllic grace, as genuinely Schubert as was ever written, is the last word of the choirs, first the knights, then the

48. "THE CONSPIRATORS," OPERA, LAST CHORUS OF KNIGHTS, C MAJOR

48. Die Verſchworenen. Oper. Letzter Ritterchor.
C-Dur

women, and, on a full C Major, hands and voices are united.

We take leave of Schubert with a brief account of "Rosamunde." The play for which he wrote the music is by Helmine Chezy. This woman has a lot to answer for. It was she who wrote the text to Weber's "Euryanthe," a libretto which effectively spoiled the opera. Schubert's fate was the same. The beautiful music (which, nevertheless, was performed) would have won contemporaneous favor if the play had not been impossible. Weber called her "that awful female." Bauernfeld said of her, "seemingly kind, somewhat ridiculous and very dirty." It is not difficult to form a mental picture of her. She was always poetising, pushing and insistent. She had come from Dresden to Vienna in the summer of 1823 and had been asked to write something for the benefit of an actress playing at the *Theater an der Wien*. The result was the play, "Rosamunde." Schubert was asked to write the music for it. But things were not so simple. First another piece called "Der böse Krollo" (The Wicked Krollo) was produced at the benefit performance. The turn of "Rosamunde" did not come before the winter. But the wickedness of Krollo pleased the public more; he put an end to the fair Rosamunde after the second performance.

After the first performance, Schwind wrote to

Schober: "Yesterday a play by that terrible Frau von Chezy was given with music by Schubert, 'Rosamunde of Cyprus.' You can imagine how gladly we all went to see it! As I had been kept at home all day on account of my cough, I could make no appointment to go with the others; at the last minute I went alone and sat in the gallery while the rest sat downstairs in the orchestra. Schubert used the overture which he had written for 'Estrella' because he thinks it is too pretentious for Estrella and will write a new one for that play. To my great joy it was received with general approval and repeated. You can imagine with what attention I followed what was happening on the stage and in the orchestra. I know that you had fears for its success. I noticed that the flute (which is given an important part) is somewhat too prominent, but that may have been the fault of the performer. Otherwise everything is understandable. After the first act a number was introduced which was not brilliant enough for the place allotted to it and had too many repetitions. A ballet was allowed to pass by without receiving any notice, and the same thing happened to the first and second intermezzi. The fact is that the audience is accustomed to start chattering right after the close of the act and it would be too much to ask them to notice such serious and excellent features. In the last act there was a chorus of shepherds and hunters so beautifully (and realistically) composed that I cannot remember ever hearing the like. There was repeated applause and I believe that this chorus will give the final blow to the chorus of Weber's 'Euryanthe.'"

Frau Chezy wrote about the play in her memoirs. The poetry was unsuitable for such an audience. The music was fairly successful. The critical opinion of the time was that Schubert, with all his originality, was, unfortunately, too bizarre. "The young man was passing through a phase of his development and one hoped that he would pass through it without harm." The sentimental ballad would surely soon become a favorite in the world of singers. Etc. etc. It seems quite remarkable that Schubert's music, in spite of everything, made such an impression. The orchestra had had only one rehearsal. It must be said that Frau Chezy was not fully satisfied and attempted a revision of her play. Schubert wrote her: "If your honor would favor me with a copy of the revised 'Rosamunde,' I would be greatly indebted." Then the play passed into oblivion and was not heard of until 1867, when Herbeck had it performed again in Vienna—that is, the music only. It still exists in this form. The music is among the most delightful of Schubert's compositions. I have told of the origin of this music in some detail because it throws light on the typical contrasts in the appraisal of Schubertian productions. Let us glance at the music itself.

The "Rosamunde" overture which we hear so often nowadays, is not the "Estrella" overture which Schubert originally used, but that of "The Magic Harp" which he considered more suitable, in spite of the fact that its themes are grounded in the form of the earlier opera. In spite of this, the overture is adroit and typical in form. The beginning (heavy chords alternating between C and D Flat) is quite in his usual manner. Then comes a charmingly turned slow tune, first appearing in E Flat Major and then in G Flat Major, finally leading to the dominant, G, and, once more, we are in the beloved C Major key. A skipping theme arises, becomes more emphatic and is entwined in close harmonies. The ground is then beaten by dancing feet. After a calming down, the lovely second theme begins, songlike in tone, turning in circles, rising higher and then calming down again. Then the third theme, with the rhythm of quarters and two-eighths, appears, ascends from pianissimo into wild gaiety, leaps and rejoices until it is carried back to the beginning.

A lively close (*vivace*) crowns a development in which all the dynamic play of light and shade reveals Schubert in every phrase.

The various numbers of 'Rosamunde" itself follow. They are like a breviary in which Schubert has recorded his favorite thoughts, which we shall examine for the last time.

What charming melancholy is breathed by the ballad! It is accompanied by stroking harmonies, resembling the music of guitars. The orchestra begins the melody in major and the voice immediately transposes it to the minor. The chords proceed in a sweet sadness; they creep past. Everything is soft and muffled. The melody consists of only a few lines, which are repeated. Minor and major alternate in Schubertian succession. The melodic contour is complete in unity. It is a fine example of a Schubert short song.

Then the "Song of the Spirits." Here is a pattern for any chorus for male voices. It is accompanied by horns and trombones, with all the strong accents *fortissimo,* the soft ones *unisono,* the transposition of harmonies, the arrangement of voices in gradation.

Nor is it different in the "Chorus of the Hunters." Here also we have four voices, but this time based on gay, virile rhythms, with all the naïveté of the romantic mood.

As a third example, there is the "Chorus of Shepherds," in the style of mixed choirs, repeating the often-used quarter with two-eighths, moving along with an easy motion, pleasantly interrupted by the solo voices and as lengthy in breath as the voice allows.

But the best of "Rosamunde" are the Intermezzi and the Ballet music. The first Intermezzo was really a revelation scarcely adapted to the popular taste of the period. Schubert cannot put enough of himself into it; he gives and gives himself here. The prelude in B Minor is nothing extraordinary. Then the main section begins, as full of delicate emotion as though it were from one of his most cherished impromptus. How deeply it is felt, how gently it breathes! This is no simple instrumental melody, this is the voice of the soul. At first it is altogether harmonic in structure with slight embellishments. But the manner in which the chords are lightly led and transposed, the way they ascend and vanish, change from the forceful minor into the soft and restrained major, is nothing less than sublime. In its variation it is attenuated and yet inexhaustible. But the music grows still more astonishing. Over a tremolo, a melody is developed in F Sharp Minor whose structure, expansion, and descending movement vividly recall Weber. Schubert delights in such themes. He is not content until he has experimented with them from every possible angle, though the different parts may suffer infinite change and transposition. Now he ascends boldly to the peaks, now he descends mysteriously in deep chords, expands and intensifies the tone into that high ecstasy which foretells the world of "Lohengrin." Again and again he uses the same themes in new keys, new combinations, new soli and new architectonics, never frightened by the strangeness of new effects that result of their own accord. He cannot arrive at the end; instead, he returns to the beginning and to the orchestra which regards him with amazement, wondering whether this symphony is to be played between two acts to an impatient and restless audience. A quick finale suppresses such speculations.

The second Intermezzo contains the undying melody which Schubert loved so much that he used it in many other pieces. In rhythm it is characteristic; a sweet, unassuming and faithfully persistent descent and ascent of a folk-tune strain, which circles around tonic and dominant till it unfolds in strange, gentle harmonies in that lovely repetition of the second part. Should mention be made at this point of the strange parallelisms of the treatment of the fifths or of the sevenths, which, at the time, caused such a commotion? No, for the truth and beauty of the expression itself are more important. Two secondary divisions are included in the repetition of the main section, but these, by their simplicity, only serve to enhance its value.

The music of the first ballet has been our companion here below and will sound in our ears even in heaven. Beloved Schubert! How often you have begun a march with a pizzicato accompaniment, arousing our curiosity, and then added to it a gaily dancing melody. But never have you achieved one more beautiful than this. How charming is the leap from G Major to A Minor and back again to G, a feat you accomplished at least a hundred times in the course of your life! How humorously the melody ascends, descends, interweaves the voices, repeats the transposition, sustains it and descends again. Now the happiest notion of all smiles at us in the midst of buzzing and beating; it dances with a rocking step; rises, giggling; makes obeisance. Surge of the folk-dance, happy pauses, harmonies of deep comprehension, and sudden, simple rejoicing—all this is written for eternity. Can this be the second ballet? It begins like the first intermezzo. Schubert, it seems, cannot have enough of it. He turns his symphony into a dance again, into a pantomime of love and transfiguration, preparing us for the farewell. This is an andante, restrained and very soft, a delicate

49. ROSAMUNDE, BALLET I, G MAJOR

49. Rosamunde. Ballett I. G-Dur

melody in which are contained all the secrets and all the joys, all the experiences and all the comforting of Schubert's spirit.

"Rosamunde" has become a symbol for us. Its fate and its appraisal are an epitome of everything that can be said of Schubert. A commission coming from an unworthy source, difficulties of performance, false judgments, going off on a side track, loss to the world, forgetfulness—these are typical of a life that had never been actually lived. But from it there rises music, secretly, almost accidentally, as a poem rises in the secret heart. It leaves earth and floats lightly through time, in the dance and song of blessèd spirits, blessing those who followed Schubert beyond his small life into his larger heaven.